Getting On in the
Creative Arts Therapies

Getting On in the Creative Arts Therapies

A Hands-On Guide to Personal and Professional Development

Erin Partridge

Foreword by Carolyn Brown Treadon

Jessica Kingsley Publishers
London and Philadelphia

First published in Great Britain in 2021 by Jessica Kingsley Publishers
An Hachette Company

1

Copyright © Erin Partridge 2021
Foreword copyright © Carolyn Brown Treadon 2021

A CIP catalogue record for this title is available from the
British Library and the Library of Congress

ISBN 978 1 78775 263 4
eISBN 978 1 78775 264 1

Printed and bound in the United States by Integrated Books International

Jessica Kingsley Publishers' policy is to use papers that are natural,
renewable and recyclable products and made from wood grown in
sustainable forests. The logging and manufacturing processes are expected
to conform to the environmental regulations of the country of origin.

Jessica Kingsley Publishers
Carmelite House
50 Victoria Embankment
London EC4Y 0DZ

www.jkp.com

Contents

Foreword

When I was approached by Erin Partridge to write the foreword for *Getting On in the Creative Arts Therapies,* I was taken aback. I have known Erin for many years, more closely in the past three as we have served on a committee together for art therapy. She is never without her art supplies and passion for the profession and individuals she serves. As an educator, clinician, and researcher, she is always looking for ways to advocate, educate, and inspire others. As we dialogued about the book and I began reading the manuscript, it led me to a retrospective reflection of my journey to becoming a professional art therapist.

For as long as I can remember, I have been creative. Painting, drawing, tearing things apart to see how they work then putting them back together, building something from scraps on the floor of my dad's workshop—I had visions of what could be. Often, the reality paled in comparison to the vision, but that drove my desire to try again and look at how something could be done differently—to tap into even more creative resources. This creativity allowed me to escape from reality for moments and at times hours on end, often returning with a refreshed soul and much lighter load.

Those early experiences prepared me to enter into the creative arts—something I knew nothing about until high school. My art teacher allowed me to come into the studio during lunch, study hall and when I had free time—this ability to escape helped make the awkward years of high school tolerable. In my junior year, she gave me a flyer about art therapy, and I knew I had found my calling.

This first domino set into play several series of events that have felt serendipitous. Talking to local art therapists provided directions in selecting educational programs that fit who I was and what I was looking for. I knew deep down I was not a professional artist, but I loved creating and found such joy in being in the studio. Knowing who you are and what you are looking for is critical to finding happiness. A good friend once told me she lived by the FranklinCovey principle (Covey, 1989): "Begin with the end in mind." When I read this book and the valuable resources it contains, that kept resonating with me—know what you want and let the decisions you make help you get closer to that goal.

Starting the process is finding the right fit for education and beginning employment. Too many times in my life, I have settled because I thought it was the right thing to do—personally and professionally. It rarely worked out, but lessons were learned. Take time to seek a program for your education where you feel comfortable, nurtured, challenged. As you seek employment, do the same—an unhealthy work environment can lead to quick and severe burnout! I teach my supervisees and students what a mentor shared with me—you take your first job because you need to work. Your second job gets you closer to your goal because you have experience and connections. These together lead you to seek where you eventually want to be.

I started my career working in day treatment with children who had severe emotional and behavioral disabilities (EBD); this was a last stop before inpatient treatment. The job led me to see the need for research in exploring how educators perceived students with EBD. Through a mentor I connected with a doctoral program. While working on my Ph.D, I started adjunct teaching and working in a nonprofit that served children, many of whom had experienced trauma and abuse. Eventually, I worked my way up to running the program and supporting interns in their field placement. After taking time off for my family, I began adjunct teaching again and serving in professional organizations. These experiences helped prepare me for the current job I hold as a graduate school program director.

All of these experiences are a process. One lesson that was hard to learn was to be patient with myself. The contributors to this book eloquently talk about this. We all make mistakes; it is part of learning. But those mistakes are opportunities for learning. It is important to understand there is a developmental process in becoming something new, and this can be very challenging, but also very exciting!

Turning back to what brought you to the creative arts in times of need is a way to practice what you preach. Early in my career, I kept in touch with my creative side, but as work and family took priority, I lost that piece of myself. It was still there, just buried. I noticed other ways creativity began to surface—building things, cooking, designing spaces—but none brought the same joy as being in the studio. We must remember to practice what we preach to remain effective at what we do: to not lose that spark that ignited us to begin our journey.

Supervision and peer support are integral to success, at all stages. Mentors have played a huge role in helping me become the art therapist and professor I am today. I still rely on them and colleagues for support and remaining connected; this is an issue when many creative arts therapists are isolated in the communities where we work. We must build each other up and serve as resources for each other.

Enhancing awareness of the creative arts is equally important. Some of the best professional connections I have are from volunteering in state and national associations and boards for art therapy. Through this work, I have been able to educate others about and advocate for creative arts therapies. Recently, I introduced an assignment I learned about through a colleague to my internship class: the elevator speech. Students have to explain what we do in 30 second or less by answering the question "Art therapy: what is that?" This is the beginning of teaching professional advocacy.

The ability to do this well appears to parallel confidence. Students who are confident in their work and themselves as arts therapists don't typically struggle as much as others. Completing the various exercises throughout this book will allow you both to reflect on who you are as an individual and a creative arts therapist, and to build your confidence in owning this identity and sharing it with others—personally and professionally. It will also help you identify who you aspire to become. Hopefully this is an ever-changing goal as you evolve professionally.

In reflecting on my personal and professional journey, I find there are more people than I can count who helped me. They taught me the importance of paying it forward. We all need each other; prospective professionals need guidance; students need mentors; and supervision is needed after graduation. It is our responsibility to help ensure the healthy future of the creative arts therapies. Everyone needs to be part of our professional evolution.

Erin has enlisted input from nine esteemed colleagues across various disciplines to share their thoughts and experiences, along with her own, on a multitude of topics ranging from beginning education to career choices and professional advocacy. Each chapter speaks to areas that prospective students, current students, young professionals, and seasoned veterans will find helpful. This book is a resource that will hold a special place in my library and one I will refer to often!

Carolyn Brown Treadon, Ph.D, ATR-BC, ATCS

Introduction

The work of creative arts therapists is varied and dynamic. Some awareness of these possibilities may be what brought you to the field and to this book. After specialized training, creative arts therapists enter into these unique professions with passion for the field and a desire to connect with and serve others through the arts. Beyond the clinical training, you need to spend time thinking and talking about the logistics of your work. Where are you willing to compromise when it comes to a job or scope of work? How do you find a good balance between things that feed your career goals and things you just accept as part of any workplace? Maybe harsh working conditions can be offset by a fabulous supervisor or well-funded training opportunities. On the other hand, perhaps a lower paycheck is bolstered by the opportunity to work with a specific client population resulting in personal fulfillment or less stress and the ability to take on special projects. Certain circumstances may work well in your early career but not later, or vice versa. You may build up skills that enable your success with complex caseloads or difficult client populations. Each person learns to navigate this path on their own terms; however, learning from the experiences of your peers and mentors can guide you towards more effective strategies along the way. Beyond reaching out to individuals, you do not have many opportunities to read or hear about the trajectory of someone's career or advice on how to change course once you have started down a path. Jess Minckley, one of the contributors to this book, created a powerful illustration of the impact of all these questions you may be confronting as you contemplate, begin, or make a shift in your career in the creative arts therapies (Figure 0.1). She described her thought process:

"Deciding" is about introspection and the process students go through as they decide which course to take. There is a heaviness to the internal process that is going on inside students. We are bombarded with information about ourselves and our families of origin, we are learning skills and theory, and we are sitting with difficult material. We write dissertations. We choose theoretical orientations. We secure practicum and internship sites, and we do those at the same time as attending classes. There's so much going on when you're in graduate school, and many times students don't have energy (or money, or time) to attend conferences, manage home life, do readings and write papers, practice self-care, and do their own therapy, let alone engage in self-advocacy at the institutional level or social justice activity. There's just not enough spoons, so decisions have to be made about where to direct one's energy (see Miserandino, 2003).

Figure 0.1 Digital drawing by Jess Minckley titled "Deciding"

Deciding what to prioritize and how to use your finite energy resources is important but difficult work. For too long, students and new professionals have been left alone in this work—you may feel some of the weight of these difficult decisions right now. Kari Rogenski offered some support around this experience:

> When I was 20 and doing my master's degree, not knowing seemed frightening. Now that I have many years of experience and I've been taught so much both from a business and a creative arts therapy perspective, not knowing is like an invitation. It makes me jazzed instead of frightened.

She offered reassurance that it will take time to feel excited or inspired by not knowing—it takes a while to develop as a clinician and feel comfortable with the "ambiguity of roles and definitions." She encouraged new professionals to dive into the experiences they encounter, finding ways to learn from each one. Regarding the self-care and balance concerns, this book contains many ways to build these practices into your life, so they do not feel like extras but rather essentials.

This book is intended to inspire and assist you. To that end, it will cover the high points of the work of creative arts therapists as well as the difficult times. Though you can gain inspiration and motivation from the successes, you also need to hear the difficult stories. Early presentations and my first book (Partridge, 2019c) were all about clinical triumphs—all my favorite stories from years of work with older adults. These are the stories we love to celebrate. However, we need to talk, write, and present about the difficulty too. The difficult professional experiences we encounter provide excellent opportunities for growth and learning; sharing these experiences helps to normalize early career struggles—times where you might feel alone in your difficulty or nervous about asking for help. I have had a few difficult conversations in my career thus far—times I have had to ask hard questions or confront dysfunction in the workplace. I have also encountered difficulty at the institutional and systemic levels. You will undoubtedly encounter hardship over the course of your career; you may not be able to avoid difficult conversations or workplace conflict entirely but you can exercise agency in how your work life evolves.

I have benefited from advice I received in my first exposure to art therapy. After finding out about the field, I was artist-in-residence for an art therapy program serving youth in a very small farming town near where I was finishing my undergraduate education. The art therapist running the program operated on the optimistic belief that if the program was meant to continue, funding would come through for us—and it did (though this was also due in no small part to her tireless grant-writing and robust research underpinning for the groups we facilitated—work I understand much more now). Over the three years I worked with her program, we expanded and contracted in response to community need and funding availability. Throughout the project's lifespan, the art therapist and I were present and available for the teens. I saw in action how flexibility enabled us to continue to meet the needs of the community we served. What I learned from her was to have hope and be open to different ways work can evolve. That openness served me well in graduate school: it empowered me to take internships outside the path I initially mapped out for myself, and I learned a great deal while navigating those different paths—lessons I put to use in my daily life 15 years later.

How to use this book

This book points to not one path, but many. It encourages exploration and self-inquiry. Though advice and examples appear throughout the text, this book asks more questions than it answers—this questioning is on purpose! On behalf of all the generous contributors, and myself, we hope it will be a resource to return to throughout your educational and professional career. Your answers to many of the questions and responses to the directives (indicated by the icons that appear throughout the book) will undoubtedly change over the course of your working life; the book is meant to guide you through the transitions you encounter across your career.

You may want to work directly in this book, or create and utilize copies in order to respond to the questions and prompts in the text. Librarians may cringe, but I encourage grangerizing (Garvey, 2013; LeGette, 2017) the book—inserting your own content through images, writing, and relevant excerpts from other sources—to really make it a scrapbook of your growth as a creative arts therapist. You also might consider creating a journal or sketchbook for your professional development as a place to explore the directives and prompts in this book along with others you encounter along your path: reflexive journaling has been described as an important part of growth and development for creative arts therapists (Barry & O'Callaghan, 2008). Returning to these same directives at different points during your professional development will offer opportunities for you to track your own evolution. For the purposes of this book, many example exercises and directives are written or visual, but please feel free to adapt and adjust the directives into the creative practice of your choice.

Icons
Throughout the book, you will encounter different icons, meant to draw your attention to a creative practice or an action you might take to interact with the book content:

Exercises and ideas that might benefit from exploring in writing.

Exercises and ideas that you can use the creative practice of your choice to explore further.

Ideas for which you may want to pause and consider deeply.

Suggestions for other reading to explore.

Topics you may want to talk through with friends, family, coworkers, supervisors, or other people in your personal and professional life.

Alerting you to something important, requiring caution or care.

Contributors
You will get to know each of the contributors and their paths as you read more about their stories in the pages of this book. Their professional experience ranges from students to people with decades

of experience in the creative arts therapies and arts therapy education. As an introduction, they provided biographical details which can be found in Appendix 1 at the back of the book.

Each contributor shared across the entire range of topics covered in this book; a main point of their contribution appears below:

Fahad al Fahed will help you learn to use language appropriate to your audience.

Fatmah Al-Qadfan will help you learn to advocate for yourself and your profession.

Tawanna Benbow will help you see how your work connects to the greater community.

Andra Duncan will help you own your role as a leader in an interdisciplinary team.

Christine Hirabayashi will help you seek the mentorship you need in your workplace.

Coleen Lorenz will help you reconnect with the work you really want to do in service of the community you want to support.

Donna Newman-Bluestein will help you learn to trust the process and try things out.

Jess Minckley will help you learn to advocate for yourself and ask important questions.

Kari Rogenski will help you identify ways to collaborate towards successes.

Hadas Weissberg will help you learn to follow where your career path leads you.

Denise Wolf will help you learn to be brave as you evolve into your professional role.

CHAPTER 1

Job Crafting and Career Trajectories

By the time someone is in leadership, publishing manuscripts, or directing training programs, they have traveled through many twists and turns in their career, but we probably do not know about those stories. These convoluted paths do not often make the keynote presentation or book jacket. By documenting the career paths of creative arts therapists at different stages of their careers in both written and expressive media, this chapter aims to explore the lived reality of work in the creative arts therapies. It introduces several general workplace and career strategies and models for advancement as interpreted and applied through the lens of creativity and the creative arts therapies.

Career paths

Two similarities came up in interviewing people about their early experiences with creative arts therapies and their discovery of the field. The first was about the importance of the arts: contributors described a lifelong love of their art form. The second similarity was about excitement over the opportunity to apply skills to something larger than their own artistic practice. Hadas Weissberg said that even though dance movement therapy was not the first thing she studied, she was "always a dancer." She studied law and became a lawyer after her service in the Israeli army because she felt she needed something more than studying dance on its own. While she was studying law, dance was always on her mind: "During my internship in law I discovered it was really not for me. I still graduated, I still became a lawyer and worked a year, but I knew I needed to change." She considered psychology, but when she found dance movement therapy she said it felt right: "This is me! This is what I'm supposed to do. I'd like to be a therapist and I have a connection to the body." Coleen Lorenz, another dance movement therapist, echoed this idea, describing how she "grew up in kinesthetic awareness." Tawanna Benbow said that while in the professional theater world, she always had an awareness of the "transformational power of theater" though she had not always known about the creative arts therapies:

> I didn't realize drama therapy was part of a larger umbrella of expressive arts or creative arts therapy, and so it was through that introduction that I realized there was a whole land of tribesmen and I was part of a village.

Her words speak to the energy of collaboration among those in the creative arts therapies, which will be discussed further in Chapter 8. She spoke about theater as essential to who she is in the world: "Theater has always been my infrastructure."

Similarly, in my own life path, I felt a pull to use my creative practice in service of something larger. I began undergraduate school as a graphic design major. In addition to working on assignments and studying, I spent a great deal of my time volunteering at the homeless shelters and raising awareness about homelessness in the city where I lived. I thought graphic design was a smart career path in the arts, but also felt called to be in service to others. Graphic design gave me some opportunities in this area; I designed the shelter's new logo and their holiday cards. But I often wished for a way to incorporate both my interests—art and working in community. When I found the field of art therapy, it seemed like the perfect fit, and as I learned more, I was sure it was what I wanted to pursue. I started looking around for more information and consumed it voraciously; the first two art therapy books I read have a place of honor on my bookshelf (*Art Is a Way of Knowing* by Pat Allen (1995) and *Art As Medicine* by Shaun McNiff (1992)). Though I was halfway through the coursework for graphic design, I made some changes, switching my major to fine art, and adding minors in women's studies and psychology. Once I completed my undergraduate degree, I went on to get a master's degree in art therapy. I have worked across the age span from birth to end of life; the oldest client I worked with was 107 when she died. After five years of clinical work, I continued my training, getting a Ph.D in art therapy. I have also incorporated other trainings along the way, including yoga teacher training and facilitation training in several specialized modalities. I teach, conduct, and supervise research, and provide group and individual therapy and art therapy supervision.

Similar to my experience, Kari Rogenski expressed a desire to devote her time to something more than the art form she studied in undergraduate school. She first learned about drama therapy while pursuing a degree in drama there. She took a week-long intensive workshop on drama therapy, which addressed some of the questions she was wondering about as a drama major:

> I had no idea what drama therapy was, and I knew I was going to be graduating with an undergraduate degree in drama and I had no interest in pursuing becoming an actor in Alberta, where I'm from. But I had no idea what I was going to do.

After learning about drama therapy at that workshop, she ordered a book online to learn more. She applied to programs and went directly from undergraduate into graduate study in drama therapy, moving from Alberta, Canada to California. After graduating, she described her career trajectory as a "very organic process," partially because of the transcontinental moves, experiences shared by other contributors in this book.

When sharing the story of her path to becoming an art therapist, Christine Hirabayashi started with her early life, describing herself in comparison to her sister: "I was the one who was quiet. I observed and I was an artist. Art was always my thing." She expressed gratitude to her parents, who never made comparisons between her interests and talents and those of her sister. She got a bachelor's degree in illustration and wanted to pursue graphic design or some other career in the arts. She made the connection between art and psychology while teaching art to children after working in a few different arts-related jobs: "It was there where I realized how art impacts kids and their confidence." She enjoyed the experience and started looking around to see what other roles she could pursue with a similar emphasis on expression and personal development through art, which led her to a graduate program in art therapy:

> I never thought I'd go back for my master's degree in anything because school was not my thing—art was my thing. But if I was going to get a degree in anything, it would be this. I'll do this.

Near the completion of her program, she started volunteering at a pain clinic, exploring different means to work with the population there. Her early work in this setting developed into a career of both clinical and community work around pain management and art therapy, doctoral research, and collaborative work with another creative arts therapist. She said that the profession is perfect for her because art was how she expressed herself and worked through different experiences in her life: "Realizing there's a thing called art therapy and I use art as my own therapy, how could I not go back to school for something like that?" Like many others, art therapy seemed right for her from the first time she heard about it.

Donna Newman-Bluestein described a similar ah-ha moment during her early adulthood. After struggling to find a job teaching English—her major in undergraduate school—she took a temporary job while she decided what to do next. A transformative experience after a dance performance led her to her life's work:

> I saw Judith Jamison performing with Alvin Ailey, and I was totally blown away with her presence on the stage. So the next night I went back and brought all my friends with me. And then again I went back the following night—so three nights in a row. And then I had a dream. I don't remember the dream; what I remember is my awakening thought, which was "I'm going to teach dance to children." And I went to work in a totally unaffiliated field and told a friend of mine, and he said, "Did you ever hear of dance therapy?" I said no and he gave me his friend's name and number, and I contacted her and I never looked back.

The "never look back" attitude was something shared among many of the interviewees for this book.

Fahad al Fahed's path illustrates finding the field through an allied profession, seeking education and advancement, and then looking forward in search of the next level of advancement and field promotion:

> Before I went into the art therapy field, I was in the art education field. I was a lecturer at King Saud University. I met a teacher who told me about art therapy and I took a lot of workshops—short educations, short training, workshops. After that I decided to do an official training to become an art therapist, and I went to NYU and graduated in 2013, then went back to teach at King Saud University for several years, and then in 2015 I went to NDNU (Notre Dame de Namur University, California) for the Ph.D program, graduating in 2018. Now I'm teaching art education at King Saud University. Some courses are relevant; I can't teach art therapy but I can give some introduction into how to look at art in different ways, but it is not what I'm looking for—I'm looking to create an art therapy master's program and hopefully it will become true.

So how do you create a program where it does not yet exist or build something large from small beginnings? There are entire shelves full of business strategy and professional development texts. The next section will cover a few ideas and practices that may be helpful in making decisions, building new roles, and reimagining the work you do.

Job crafting

The term "job crafting" was coined by researchers looking at a more holistic picture of work—beyond just the job description or employee traits (Wrzesniewski, Berg, & Dutton, 2010; Wrzesniewski & Dutton, 2001). The idea of job crafting is well suited to creative arts therapists, as it works with the metaphor of creation or making. Denise Wolf described how she frames her full, color-coded calendar to her students as "part of the creative process, building a career rather than having a job." The work people do and the interactions people have at work "that compose the days, the jobs, and, ultimately, the lives of employees are the raw materials employees use to construct their jobs" (Wrzesniewski & Dutton, 2001, p. 179). Some of your "raw materials" are requirements of the setting and your role—you may have documentation requirements or assigned group meetings. Your interactions may be primarily with clients or may encompass a whole network of care providers and other professionals. Some of your other raw materials include your creativity, curiosity, training in various modalities, and ability to work both verbally and nonverbally.

As a creative arts therapist, you have so many skills that may go untapped because you are operating within the confines of an existing job description. Or you may see unmet needs you could address through a realignment of your scope of work. Additionally, you can get involved in job crafting as a means of addressing systemic injustice in the organizational structures you work within: "creating new narratives and paradigms of practice" (Nolan, 2019, p. 77) in order to better serve your communities. Kuther and Morgan (2020) created a long list of transferable skills people with a background in psychological training have, including knowledge of human behavior, research, critical thinking, idea synthesis skills, adaptability, and efficacy at communication and other interpersonal interactions. These skillsets can open doors to roles outside the traditional clinical world; some of these opportunities will be discussed in Chapters 4, 6, and 7.

Job Description Analysis

Take some time to examine your written job description (or a job description you can get a copy of if you are a student).

What elements of the job description as written make you excited about your role?

Are there tasks or responsibilities you regularly do that are not captured by the description as it is currently written?

What edits would you make to your job description if you had the opportunity?

Exerting some control over your work life can help you feel more motivated. Fosslien and Duffy (2019) suggested that it is possible, "even in constrained professional situations, to create moments of freedom and inspiration" (p. 53). Having an eye or ear tuned to possibilities for freedom can reveal opportunities. Where might a few moments to improvise with your instrument increase your sense of satisfaction at the end of a work day? How can you make space for a brief creative break between sessions to enliven yourself? Is there time and space for movement in your day? Consider putting these mini-breaks on your work calendar or setting recurring alerts on your phone. Gillam (2018) wondered if opportunities for creativity in the daily work life of mental health providers might "provide workers with satisfying opportunities to be creative, so they were no longer overwhelmed by narrowness and mechanicalness and forced to satisfy their need for creativity elsewhere" (p. 22). If work currently feels mechanical or boring, see how you can apply job crafting techniques to make it more rewarding and alter the narrative about your work life.

As a creative arts therapist, you have an advantage over many other professions; you are skilled at working with constraint, innovating, and dreaming up new approaches to the circumstances at hand.

Time management

There is ample literature and professional advice out in the world about time management and trainings you can pursue in project management systems. In a review of best practices, Sopon (2017) identified five major time management techniques used in academic settings: self-management, timing, urgent-important matrix, Pomodoro, and Pareto's method. These techniques were each accompanied by practices and strategies. Creative arts therapists should think about how these might apply not only to the day-to-day of our education and jobs but also to our creative lives. If you struggle with time management, take some comfort that there are many tools to assist you. Another reassurance comes from a study of the time management strategies of medical providers; the researchers found that experienced physicians used time management tools and techniques that could be easily taught, as well as relying on time management practices based on tacit knowledge gained through their years of practice (Kleshinski, Dunn, & Kleshinski, 2010). You too will improve in your time management and balancing abilities as you gain experience and exposure to a wide range of techniques. Your work will start to have a pattern or rhythm as you learn how to structure your time and your energy towards the different priorities of your career.

📖 Time and Project Management

Look into the literature about time management and project management. There are many different approaches to try. Experiment with the different techniques to find the one that works for you.

Hint: Try both digital and analog tools and strategies.

One practice that has been incredibly valuable for me is to implement a reading hour at the end of most work days. I schedule it into my calendar and mark myself as busy during that time. I use the hour to read new journal articles or books relevant to my work or to our current lines of research. Since implementing this practice, I have realized several different benefits to building this ritual into the last hour of my work days. I end the day with a dose of inspiration or curiosity, which continues into my commute. This closing hour for my work day is much healthier than ending the day with frantic emails or having to step away from my desk with unfinished tasks. When I get in my car to drive home, I can more easily disconnect from work. As a salaried employee and early-riser, it also ensures I will leave instead of slowly adding more hours to my day. After several years of this practice, I definitely notice when I cannot keep this schedule—it has become an important part of my day.

Ritual

Another way to think about making space at work is through the use of ritual. In a book covering the research and application of ritual in the workplace, the authors connected the use of ritual to create better individual, team, and system-wide experiences at work; they drew a direct connection between effective rituals and creativity:

Can you be an architect of your life? Even if you are not the manager of your company or your team, you can use lightweight strategies—like rituals—to make work more like you wish it could be. This means bringing a sense of practical creativity to work life. (Ozenc & Hagan, 2019, p. xxv)

The authors suggested trying different rituals to address problems and to work towards a better understanding of the type of work you want to do in the world. These ideas connect to Dissanayake's (1995) writing about the long history of human use of ritual to understand our world and connect with each other. Paradoxically, the structure of ritual may enable you to think more expansively about your role and your work and to come up with new ways to inhabit your professional self. Kari Rogenski spoke about the importance of ritual in her work life. She said she keeps books or decks of inspiration cards around in her desk and office as a means of grounding and inspiration:

I can quickly draw a card, take a deep breath, take a moment, and slow myself down. Maybe I have five minutes or maybe I have two, but making sure those rituals are part of my every day is extremely important.

She said that even though the time towards this ritual is short, she always feels inspired by it and likes that it helps to shift her perspective. Workplace rituals do not need to take up a lot of time and do not need to be fancy to have an impact.

Stretch yourself

Tawanna Benbow connected the work of job crafting to the ongoing dynamic work of creative people. In her advice for creative arts therapists, she encouraged an entrepreneurial spirit:

I just would encourage that trailblazing mentality. Do not be afraid to begin to walk and to start to chart a path that is not charted already. Do not be afraid to be a trailblazer. That's what the heart of our work is—it is about self-expression and creativity and you just have to go, you just have to step out!

Job crafting may involve stretching yourself. Being brave enough to request additional training or responsibility. Applying for a new role. Starting something new. Initiating a collaboration. You need to look for paths that do not yet exist and take the first steps to bring that path into being.

◎ Trailblazing Exploration

You can explore the idea of trailblazing in any media you choose. Consider working in an art form that is not your primary way to express yourself—doing so may bring new or unexpected ideas to the surface. This creative exploration might work really well as a comic or piece of sequential art (see Chapter 3).

Imagine the terrain you will travel through.

Are there parallel or nearby paths you can look to as examples?

When you think about creating a path for yourself, what tools do you have currently? What additional tools do you need?

Are there people available to guide you along the way?

Do any maps or navigation systems exist to help you? What do those look like?

What is the weather like along this path?

How will you know when you have reached your destination?

Seeking balance

As much as you might want to avoid endless paperwork or bureaucracy, these tasks are a reality for most people's work lives. Job crafting is not the elimination of all the difficult or frustrating parts of our jobs, the "outside parts" as Christine Hirabayashi described them. Instead, it enables you to influence and shape how you spend your work life, placing greater emphasis on things where you find meaning.

As Coleen Lorenz described her work trajectory, her story seemed to involve several threads of ideas pulling her towards the integrative work she does today. Always interested in the mind–body connection, she began studying the way "what we think affects our physiology." When she transitioned into a role as a clinical supervisor, she described a setting where she had greater clinical risks put upon her in a system that was not supporting her: "It felt larger than me. The system was very sad." She did a combination of different kinds of clinical work in different settings for a while and then she wanted to get back into a full-time job: "Dance called me back in an artistic way." Her next transition enabled a return to her creative and artistic roots; she got a position in a university running the dance program and teaching at a local high school. She was able to incorporate dance therapy into the work with students. Unfortunately, the university eliminated all the visual and performing arts—time for another transition. Her current scope of work includes continued teaching of dance and psychology at the high school and running a nonprofit focused on dance therapy, art, wellness, and yoga. Returning to the more artistic, expressive, less clinical role enabled her to create a work life for herself that prioritizes access to individual and community wellness. She is also the artistic director of a dance company doing storytelling performances around psychological issues: "My greatest joy is taking the abstractness of the art side and embedding it with the truths that are out there around neuropsychology."

Christine Hirabayashi talked about finding balance by "staying focused on the work with the patients" as a way to overcome some of the other difficulties of working in a system. Making the decision to add private practice work to her plate was another way for her to have more control and autonomy over her day and to continue to grow and develop as a clinician:

> Knowing that I have a specialty, pushing myself to see what else is there. I could stay at the clinic forever and keep building programs, but I feel like I have more to offer. I love it. I've always worked with adults with chronic pain. And now I see children, teens, adults—some with chronic pain, some just contemplating where they are in life. I am still working existentially, but I am able to do it in a new way. Not just pigeonholing me with a population. It's made me want to be curious about other things. How can I be creative in working with other populations?

Sometimes balance comes sequentially as you transition from one role to the next, and sometimes you can create balance by restructuring time spent in multiple roles. You may even be able to create balance in a single workplace through strategic approaches to your caseload. For example, when I worked in a setting with both art therapy treatment groups and art for leisure groups, we were able to balance our assignments between treatment and leisure group facilitation across the work-week. Later, in working with older adults, I structured my week to include a variety of verbal and nonverbal groups working in different levels of care. I tried to keep my schedule balanced, considering the preparation time, energy expenditure, and clean-up work for each group and setting in mind when I built the calendar. Find balance where you can—work with your supervisor or coworkers to find as much balance as possible for each of you.

When Andra Duncan and I worked in the same older adult care setting, we realized we needed to advocate for restructuring our groups. We both worked in all three areas of the building—skilled nursing, memory care, and assisted and independent living. Over time, as we added groups to the calendars, we also added stress and difficult transition times. In order to rebalance the calendar, we met with our supervisor at a big conference room table. We wrote each group we facilitated on individual sticky notes and used the large space of the table to reorganize our week. As we worked, we thought about balancing our time, creating an even distribution of art therapy and music therapy in all the program areas, and creating less hectic schedules for ourselves. The resulting calendar was much more manageable and well worth the hour of work to rethink things.

⌨ Workplace Balance

Invite your peers to come together or ask your supervisor about having a conversation with your team about balance.

Bring copies of your schedules, blank calendars, sticky notes, and plenty of writing tools.

Invite everyone to think about their best and worst days at work. Consider everything that goes into each day, including the transitions between groups or sessions, the room usage, the content covered, documentation requirements, etc.

Invite everyone to think about their personal cognitive, emotional, and physiological needs too. For example, a self-identified "morning person" may do better when tasks requiring more mental sharpness are scheduled earlier in the day. Or someone else may have a fast metabolism and tend to have difficulty when lunch break is delayed by a group that always runs overtime. Both of these concerns can be addressed through simple scheduling adjustments.

As you review your personal needs for balance, take the time to look at how clients' needs for balance are or are not being met—oftentimes groups, sessions, and other activities get added to calendars at different times by different people without considering how it impacts individual clients.

If you are in private practice or are the sole person responsible for the calendar, you could lay out the week or month calendar with a short description of each client, group, or task. Though you may not be able to reschedule all your individual clients, you may be able to shift some of the non-client contact time or set some scheduling goals for the future (for example, gradually shifting away from evening sessions or moving all your group work to the afternoons).

Mapping your career

Many of us use timelines with our clients in therapy as a way to understand their lives and plan for the future; timelines are relevant to considering our careers as well. A professional timeline includes elements that may appear on a CV or resume as well as other significant life events. As you imagine into the future, where do you see your career heading? How will life events shape your path?

◎ Career Path Directive _____

Create a timeline of your educational, work, and professional experiences. Be sure to indicate times of transition. What were your emotions like at that time? What did you learn about yourself in that transitional period?

When representing different milestones, indicate what you learned in each situation and how you carried that learning into the next opportunity. Likewise, represent obstacles you faced. Were they inter- or intrapersonal? Did you face systemic barriers? What did you learn from confronting those barriers?

Where and how have luck or "happy accidents" factored into where you are today?

If you are currently a student, project into the future: What do you hope for yourself? What worries do you have about your future career?

Who have been your teachers and mentors along the way? What of them have you carried forward?

Where have you had opportunities to teach and mentor others?

You might use a life path directive to think in a more abstract fashion. What are you looking forward to? What excites you? The image in Figure 1.1 began in my art journal and evolved with digital editing. I created it while traveling abroad to the European Consortium for Arts Therapies Education conference; I was inspired by the vast network of people attending and by the potential to engage more deeply with my international colleagues. At the time I was creating the image, I did not have a sense for what my future in international travel and collaboration would be, but wanted to explore that idea in art.

When you are just beginning to contemplate what you want to do in your career, it can feel daunting. It is important to remember that you do not have to make a "forever choice" right away. You can explore many different choices over the course of your career. Christine Hirabayashi reflected on the creative space she has had to develop and evolve her practice: "They allowed me the creative space to think more openly and to make something different and of my own." When asked how to ask for that space, she immediately recommended that you should write it up as a formal business proposal, answering any questions decision-makers might have and focusing on the need the idea addresses. She said her success came from making it very easy for the people in power to say yes.

*Figure 1.1 "My Role As a Navigator"—mixed media on
paper, edited with several digital art applications*

Coleen Lorenz had beautiful advice for navigating your winding path
as a student or new professional: "Explore the paths. Let your heart
lead the way." Explore in whatever way makes sense in your life. Some
of this exploration will be your own employment and some will be
vicarious; when exploring via a mixed-employment portfolio is not
feasible, read the published literature focusing on populations you have
not yet encountered or covering ways of working you have not had a
chance to try yet.

CHAPTER 2

Training and
Academic Work

Once you have discovered your arts therapy field, it is time to choose a training program or academic institution. This chapter covers strategies for choosing training programs and makes recommendations for thriving in school, including relationship development, professional practices, and conference attendance.

Which training program?

As with any higher education choices, there are multiple factors to consider. The international, national, and regional organizations relevant to your desired creative arts therapy field have resources for preparing to choose and enter training. The accreditation and alignment of the programs are important to take into consideration. Your study is "not merely the learning of directives, activities or techniques but rather a nuanced rendering of careful, in-depth integration of art and psychology with a large dose of personal, increasing self-awareness" (Junge & Newall, 2015, p. 29). Additionally, thinking about the other areas of your life and how graduate training will work, given obligations, interests, and needs, is important. The comparison chart provided leaves room for you to compare several graduate training options with keeping things status quo. You might also consider comparisons with pursuing other paths. These alternate comparisons are not meant to discourage pursuing a career in the creative arts therapies but rather to illuminate previously unconsidered concerns or needs. Junge and Newall (2015) strongly encouraged reading and personal exploration prior to beginning study in the creative arts therapies, and this exercise should help with some of that exploration.

When visiting campuses, inquire about sitting in on a class and meeting current students and professors. Visit the library, dining hall, and other campus amenities—can you picture yourself in this setting? Inquire about seeing or testing out the online learning platforms in use for courses. Ask about student jobs, financial aid, student health insurance, and other important considerations with financial implications. Get as much information as you can about the real cost of attending—factoring in things like books, materials, additional training requirements, and commuting time and cost. The more information you have, the better prepared you will be to make an informed decision.

No matter how much you prepare and do research, there may still be some question marks in your mind when you begin your education in creative arts therapy. Jess Minckley's work (Figure 2.1) illustrates "the sometimes confusing, circuitous path to becoming an art therapist." She reminds us too that "once inside the higher education and professional domains, there are choices one must make about personal values, theoretical orientation, professional ethics, etc." Kari Rogenski, reflecting back on the period of time just prior to completing her undergraduate degree but before starting graduate training in drama therapy, experienced some of the questions Jess Minckley identified. After the initial inspiration from the workshop, and as a response to the pressure she felt to decide what she was going to do with her life, she applied to graduate school: "I didn't know where I was going to go, how I was going to live, or how I was going to pay for it." She described herself at the time as having little professional or life experience as an adult—she graduated at a very young age. Each of the choices along the way can feel overwhelming—which program to enter, how to select an internship site, what kind of research to pursue for your thesis or capstone. Taking both a systematic and linear and an arts-based approach to making these decisions can really help you feel more comfortable with your choices.

Comparison Chart for Graduate Training Programs

	Program 1	Program 2	Program 3	Other Field of Study	Status Quo
Name					
Location					
Duration					
Traditional/low-residency/online					
Degree					
Credential/license					
Internship/practicum placement					
Job placement					
Population access					
Specialization opportunities					
Opportunities for advancement					
Postgrad support and community					
Other aspects to consider					

*Figure 2.1 "Deciding which direction to take"—
digital illustration by Jess Minckley*

Portability of licensure and certification

One of the practical matters you need to consider when choosing a program relates to licensure and the portability of your training. While it might seem exciting to move to a new state, region, or country for graduate school or continued training, will your investment of time and energy translate back to the place you want to live in long term? It is not impossible to move once you have started on the path of training or licensure, but it can get complicated.

 It is helpful to ask yourself: Where do I want to take my creative arts therapy practice and what do I need to practice there?

Making a decision

Fatmah Al-Qadfan described her journey from early awareness of the field through selecting a program:

> I didn't know about the creative arts therapies until I was well out of college! I was working at a local museum and cultural center when I came across a documentary about drama therapy with inmates in one of the prisons in Lebanon. That documentary was my introduction to the creative arts therapies in general, and drama therapy in particular. After watching the documentary, I knew this was something I wanted to pursue, and began the search for training programs and graduate programs in earnest. I selected a handful of programs in the US and a couple of them wrote back to say that they could not offer funding for an international student. I selected Kansas State University because the program is led by an incredible woman called Sally Bailey, who wholeheartedly believes in drama therapy and creates internships and funding opportunities for students in her program. After an email exchange, I called Sally on the phone and she really encouraged me to apply to K-State. I wanted to make sure that the program and the school were a good fit for me, so even after I got accepted, I traveled there to meet students and get a feel for the program. My academic experience at Kansas State University was very rewarding, and I was given some flexibility to hone my skills in the theater arts as well as being a therapist. I felt supported in designing a program of study that met my needs.

Fatmah Al-Qadfan's story demonstrates both proactivity by the student and varied levels of support from the programs she considered.

Making the most of it

Student mindset

Selecting the "right" program may be less important than one's attitude once admitted. Among those interviewed for this book, many cited a need for student openness as a means to take advantage of educational opportunities. Similarly, Lindvang (2013) wrote that therapists need to "meet the complex reality of the therapy world with openness and flexibility" (p. 24). Regarding this idea of openness, Donna Newman-Bluestein acknowledged that we often pursue the things that we already feel interested in or open to. She suggested self-observation and testing these belief systems:

> What in the world, what out there in the world do I open to and what do I shut down from? Noticing those. What am I closed to that I might consider opening to? Maybe I can put my toe in the water.

Learn as much as you can from everyone you encounter on your path. Nurture your critical-thinking, lifelong-learning self—you will benefit from growing this part of yourself in your future professional life. Developing a hunger for new knowledge will support your continuing education, professional development and advancement, and possible research.

◎ Openness Exploration _____

What does openness to new ideas mean to you?

How does this open-self sound?

Imagine the gesture and stance of this open, ready-for-learning part of yourself.

How does this self stand?

How does this self present to the world?

You may choose to explore this open posture/gesture in movement, sound, or visual imagery.

_____

Openness can help you find the path you are meant to be on. Christine Hirabayashi described how her openness led to her current professional satisfaction: "Organically, the next step led to the next step and the next step; it was just about pushing and challenging myself." Likewise, openness can make it a little easier to transition away from something that is not working or where you are no longer growing. Being open to letting go of things you thought were "permanent" or long term can expose you to new opportunities. When I made the decision to move across the country for graduate school, I was thinking of it as a permanent move. I thoroughly enjoyed my experience in New York, and I believe I encountered growth and development opportunities I would not have had otherwise. But when family and an exciting next step for my career called me back to California, I was open to making another big change. This openness resulted in more stability in my career, meeting many new colleagues, professional development, and ultimately openness to the next phase of my life. Denise Wolf recommended bringing the improv rule of "yes, and..." to your career; she described how in her own life she wanted to build a career around art therapy and education while making space for the "random opportunities that present themselves." You will grow and change a great deal as you become a creative arts therapist. Be open to how your life will evolve post-graduation.

How do you learn?

Graduate school is an excellent time to interrogate old belief systems about your academic past. In a review of the evidence about learning styles, Pashler, McDaniel, Rohrer, and Bjork (2008) found little to no support for common classifications of learning styles: "There is growing evidence that people hold beliefs about how they learn that are faulty in various ways, which frequently lead people to manage their own learning and teach others in nonoptimal ways" (p. 117). Instead of labeling yourself based on areas of struggle, think about what has helped you to be successful in the past.

 Learning Exploration _____

What works well for you?

Do you like to work independently or do you enjoy thinking things through out loud or through participation in group work?

Do you generally ask questions aloud in the moment, or do you prefer to follow up later with the instructor?

Where do you need to be challenged?

What kind of feedback helps you to grow?

Hint: Your answers to these questions can also be useful to share when you begin a new internship or work placement.

Being aware of what helps you succeed can enable you to be more proactive about getting what you want and need out of the classroom. Participation in group activities is a common element of classes for training in the creative arts therapies. However, not every student is comfortable in highly interactive learning environments. In an exploration of student silence in the classroom, Reda (2009) discovered that speaking or not speaking in class is far more complicated than it may seem: "Students understand their own silences in far more complicated ways than we do, often seeing multiple causes and issues at play in a teacher's request for oral participation and their decisions to speak or not" (p. 7). Silence has many causes. It might be socially or culturally informed, a sign of deep listening, a symptom of exhaustion or anxiety, or feelings of imposter syndrome. Reflecting on imposter phenomena in graduate training for dance therapists, Mason (2009) described the silence of her peers:

> During seminars, my female peers often remain silent, rather than confidently argue their viewpoints or challenge theoretical perspectives. In discussions with colleagues after the seminar, I found out that the lack of engagement is often due to the fact that these colleagues did not feel they could adequately express and defend their viewpoints. (p. 20)

She identified fears of being wrong and using unfamiliar language as some of the barriers to speaking up in class. Programs and individual professors should be addressing these concerns by structuring training to meet the needs of students, particularly given the growing discourse around critical pedagogy in the arts therapies (Gipson, 2015; Talwar, 2019a).[1] Allen (1995) suggested creating caricatured images as a means to explore feelings triggered by power dynamics. Understanding your

---

1   See also www.criticalpedagogyartstherapies.com

learning needs will help you make choices about training and then to advocate for yourself once you are in a program.

Work ethic

None of us can be the perfect, present student all the time, but the more care and attention you give to your training, the better prepared and more self-aware clinician you will become. You will not retain every bit of information from every class you take, but you will live your way into your new professional self. Developing a good work ethic while you are in school will help you in your clinical world: deadlines do not disappear post-graduation; charts and case notes have to be done; training and continuing education have deadlines and timelines. Efficacy at juggling multiple stressors is an essential skill to build up while in training or graduate school. It might be useful to create some sort of tracking system for yourself. Explore times where you are overwhelmed or fall behind in your work and try to identify how to avoid those things in the future.

 When You Are Overwhelmed... _____

Are there any factors that predispose you to feeling overwhelmed?

What led up to the overwhelming situation?

What is keeping you stuck?

What will help you make changes?

_____

There is not one perfect solution for developing your best work ethic. Some people thrive by breaking tasks down into daily goals, while others like to keep the day-to-day more flexible with their eyes on the long-term goals. Some need accountability partners, others self-motivate. Explore different approaches and find things that serve you well. Return to the suggestions in Chapter 1 about time management.

Even as you develop openness and a work ethic, you also deserve to be supported and challenged by your academic work. Denise Wolf shared that part of how she thinks about supporting this work as an educator: by "teaching through process and content." She said that it is not just about what she teaches—the information she provides in class—but also about how she provides the content and how the students receive it. As Junge wisely stated, "education to become an art therapist should be transformative and life changing" (Junge & Newall, 2015, p. ix). It will also require being introspective and considering yourself as not just a clinician but also a complex human, as Gold (2012) described in music therapy training. You will need support in doing this transformative, human work. Create as robust a supportive environment as possible for your process, including time for play, creativity, and exploration.

Therapy for the student therapist

Engaging in your own therapy during training is an important part of self-study and the process of evolving into a self-aware clinician. Some programs require students to be in their own therapy, while others make strong recommendations; in a study of undergraduate music therapy program coordinators in the United States, 14 percent of study participants reported that their program required personal therapy and 32 percent encouraged it (Gardstrom & Jackson, 2011). Other training programs and regional or national requirements differ—some requiring it prior to eligibility for licensure or certification. Seeing a therapist is also a good pattern to establish for longevity in the field and to develop as a clinician (Digiuni, Jones, & Camic, 2013). Lindvang (2013) described the potential for self-development through personal therapy incorporated into a music therapy training program. It is important to make time to work with your lived experiences and process new ideas and associations stimulated by course content and client contact, and to develop healthy coping skills for your future.

Though many graduate programs provide time and space for self-exploration as part of the coursework, it is not necessarily appropriate to bring the deep process work you can do in individual therapy into your classroom or supervision. Furthermore, therapy is an excellent support for the stressors of graduate education. In reflecting on her time as a student, Kim Newall described some of what individual therapy for therapists in training can address:

Student anxiety levels spike, tears flow, tempers flare, and depression hits as old personal material surfaces. Each of us travels in both a public space of academic requirements and developing professionalism, and also in private worlds that toss old patterns like stinking garbage into our faces. (Junge & Newall, 2015, p. 5)

Look for affordable, convenient options at your student health or counseling center or inquire about referrals to community resources. If possible, seek out the services of a creative arts therapist—you might even explore working with a creative arts therapist of a different discipline than your own. Alternatively or additionally, you might begin a journaling process as a way to track your emotions and experiences during school and training; a study of reflexive journaling by music therapy students (Barry & O'Callaghan, 2008) found a range of uses and benefits to the practice.

Academic relationships

Your peers and professors in your creative arts therapy training are the beginnings of your professional network.

As you transition from student to professional, your professors will form part of this network as well. They will be there through the difficult and stressful times; they may help you locate internship and job leads in the future; and they will be friendly faces in the crowd at professional conferences. When you are evaluating potential training programs, consider how many students will be in your classes, how much access you will have to your professors and advisors, and what postgraduate support will look like. Remember, you are not just deciding where to study, but also making decisions that will impact your future professional network.

Support During and After Study

Understanding the logistical and support opportunities each program offers is important. What access do they offer to networking, job placement, and lines of research? Read publications by the professors teaching in the program—do you feel a sense of alignment with or curiosity about their ideas? Does the school incorporate visiting lecturers? Between the faculty, programming, and location, is there a diversity of ideas, approaches, and philosophies available to you? Looking ahead beyond graduation, is there a robust alumni network for postgraduate support? How is the program networked with the rest of the campus community? Some programs have many opportunities for students from varied backgrounds to interact.

From training into the real world

It can be difficult to conceptualize what you will do as a creative arts therapist in the early phases of your education. However, once you begin observing or doing the work, it can come alive. Hadas Weissberg described the shift from uncertainty in her first months in a dance movement therapy program to more self-assuredness when she started her practicum:

> In the beginning I felt like, I don't really know what I'm supposed to do. I really enjoyed the experience, and felt like it was a lot of work on myself. My classmates—we were all very confused. When we got to practicum, things got better. We had a really good supervisor. I feel like I was confused until I started working.

More questions will come up as you gain exposure to clients in fieldwork and practicum and as you learn more about your field. When asked about students' questions and uncertainty directly, Denise Wolf said that one of the most common questions she gets from students is "How do you know what to say?" She said that she believes this question is part of their developing a framework for understanding the whole picture of their future roles as art therapists:

They're building a house of art therapy. And they want to know, where are the studs? And where are the windows? And it is much more smooshy or liminal than that. And I am working on finding a way to communicate that to them.

In the beginning of your career or when you have transitioned to work with a different population, you will feel a desire for more clear-cut answers: if my client does x, I respond with y. Unfortunately, one of the difficult parts of our work with other people is that we cannot rely on manuals and simple equations alone. It is also one of the beautiful and dynamic things about the work. Merino (2020) described a need for balance between the theoretical part of teaching and the encouragement of flexible and adaptive responses to clients—it is not easy to find this balance when teaching! Some of the answers to the "How do you know what to say?" question Denise Wolf identified are that it will develop over time and to trust the process—answers she acknowledges do not always feel satisfying in the moment. She also normalizes the experience of making mistakes, which she described as "a beautiful opportunity to make repairs with yourself and with the client or clients, and model it as a parallel process—how do you grow, how do you recover from that?" She encourages her students to not be afraid and to lean into this growth opportunity.

Denise Wolf describes the space between training and education in the creative arts therapies and practice as a "gray space." She elaborated on this idea:

They sit in our classes, they learn all this stuff, and then they go out in the field and think, "Well, this isn't how I read it in the book" or "This isn't how we talked about it in class," and they ask "How do I navigate this space?"

She suggested that educators and supervising clinicians need to create a language to talk about all the different ways the actual practice of art therapy looks in the real world.

As you move through your education, keep all conduits of information open to absorbing the stories you hear from professors and supervisors. Think about the type of creative arts therapist you want to become, and seek out support and knowledge that will further your interests. Most importantly, ask questions. Your questions will support not only your own growth and development but also the development of your classmates, your teachers, and the field.

CHAPTER 3

Early Work Experience

This chapter outlines the early work experiences of different creative arts therapists and proposes some ways to approach the job search and early-career decisions. Your first few jobs can be very influential in the path your career takes. That said, you do not need to know exactly what you want to do for the rest of your life right away; in many ways, your training continues as you move through your early work experiences.

First steps in your career

Donna Newman-Bluestein had some excellent advice for your first few rounds of job-seeking; she recommended a balance between knowing your own needs and wishes and also taking some risk by taking a first step:

> Really believing in ourselves, trusting ourselves, doing the best that we can to know ourselves. Having a vision and taking a step. "I don't know if this job is going to be right for me, but I'll apply for it."

Your early internships and first jobs will help you gain clarity about what you want as your career evolves.

Job-seeking, especially as a new graduate, can feel overwhelming. The pressure to find *something* can lead to a feeling that you have to accept *anything*. In reflecting on her first job searches and employment, Fatmah Al-Qadfan recommended new graduates seek employment "at a place that has one or more creative arts therapists because the transition from graduate school to work is not easy, and it helps to have someone show us the ropes." I wholeheartedly agree—my first two jobs post-graduation were in settings with many creative arts therapists of different disciplines, and it prepared me for moving into positions later in my career where I was the only art therapist in the setting and I needed to be more of an advocate for the field. Clarifying goals and needs prior to accepting a job or even before going out on interviews is helpful. Donna Newman-Bluestein was clear about what she wanted in a work environment: "One thing that I've always wanted to do is to work in institutions. I wanted to work in places where there was peer support. Where I could learn from others and they could hear my perspectives." When possible, working with others from your discipline or at least with other creative arts therapists creates opportunity for camaraderie and support.

The reality of our lives does sometimes dictate that we have to take the best job available to us at the time. Kari Rogenski spoke about her circumstances immediately after graduating: "I went directly from grad school to being a very in-debt new professional who needed a job. So I applied for anything and everything I could get my fingers on." She ended up doing work in community mental health that did contribute to her career, and she was able to do some of the work of drama therapy in those roles, but she laughed as she recalled her early job titles. Even when you are in a less-than-ideal role or a setting that was not your first or even fifth choice, find ways to think about your work as a learning opportunity. Get as much as you can from the role, while you seek your next stepping stone.

Having a sense, pre-interview, of what you need and want from your first professional role can help you formulate questions to ask and to evaluate potential employers. Try to get as much information as possible when in the interview process. Do not be afraid to ask questions about what your day-to-day schedule will entail, how you will be supported, and where you will have opportunities to grow. As Christine Hirabayashi said, "They're not just interviewing you for a job: you're interviewing them to see if it is a good fit." She recommended coming to the interview with this attitude as well as an eye for how you might grow in the position.

Interview Questions

Think about what you might want to ask, prior to arriving at a job interview. Consider what helps you feel comfortable in a working environment and ask questions relevant to those needs. Think about your career goals and questions that will assist you in determining if this role moves you closer to these goals. Having a few questions ready to go will help you feel confident and prepared if and when you are asked whether you have questions.

Denise Wolf endorsed the need for regular on-site supervision as part of an ideal first job along with other forms of professional development. She suggested seeking opportunities for the new clinician to observe other creative arts therapists and other verbal therapies—to gain exposure to different ways of working. In addition to exposure, these observations would enable new clinicians in "developing a shared language" with the other therapists and professionals in the setting. She also spoke about the importance of exposure to both group and individual work so that you do not feel pigeon-holed in your early career and turn down later opportunities just because you have not had exposure to them.

As she thought about what an ideal first job for a drama therapist would be, Kari Rogenski specified that the setting would need to recognize that the person was a mental health provider: "I think one of the mistakes we see in elder care today in continuing care communities is that their directors of programming aren't licensed or trained professionals." She did actually have a positive work experience in life enrichment for older adults, which she remembered fondly:

> If I could have picked anything, I don't think I would have changed my first job when I moved back to California. That to me was a dream job! I was leading groups, I was doing one-to-ones, I was learning to be a supervisor and a manager. There were so many components of the job that were healthy and excellent.

When thinking about what she did not have, she mentioned not having a "community of therapists" and mentorship or support towards her licensure. She said it would otherwise be the perfect job as a new graduate, giving them the ability to "dive into some structure, but with a lot of respect and focus on the therapeutic side of programming for older adults."

The role of a creative arts therapist can look different depending on the context; where you work will influence how you work. Edwards (2004) stated:

> [T]heir practice will also be influenced by the particular needs of the client group with whom they work and by the institutional context within which this work takes place. Obvious though it may be to say so, the therapeutic needs of troubled children are often very different from those of adult psychiatric patients. Moreover, the experience of working as a member of a small team providing a specialised service to a particular client group can be very different to that of working single-handed in a large organisation where the client group may be more varied. Each situation presents the art therapist with its own particular challenges, and what may be appropriate in one setting can be quite unsuitable in another. Consequently, art therapists have developed diverse ways of working according to their area of specialisation. (p. 79)

Creative arts therapists adapt approaches to fit the clients and the setting. One excellent example of this adaptation to fit the context comes from my work at a large state hospital with individuals who committed sex offenses. For safety reasons, all therapeutic and leisure groups were facilitated by two staff. It was an incredible learning experience to co-lead groups with other therapists, many times with different training and philosophies from my own. My style is very process-oriented and frequently nonverbal, and I often facilitated with highly verbal therapists; learning to balance our approaches helped me to learn new skills and appreciate and strengthen my own therapeutic practices. My first few groups felt awkward—sometimes I wished a co-facilitator would speak less or that we could interact differently. There was also an overlay of anxiety about the setting, especially knowing that the individuals often tested new staff. But as we would get to know each other, we found ways for our different approaches to complement each other.

Similar to the recommendations about choosing a school, if possible ask to observe a group or to see as much as possible of the work environment. Pay attention to warning signs when you are interviewing. Sometimes they are subtle and sometimes they are giant flashing lights. My very first interview post-graduation for a therapeutic after-school program began with the interviewer stashing me in a classroom and locking me in while he went to deal with a crisis. He explained that there was no one else to do it and was flustered when he returned almost an hour later, so much so he had trouble focusing on the interview. I was also on-edge, having spent an hour locked in an unfamiliar place with limited information. Though I really needed a job, when considering the pay, commute, and my observations during the interview, I decided to pass when the job was offered to me; the compensation did not offset the other difficulties. In contrast, though I was left waiting for over an hour prior to an interview for another job a few years later, the other things I observed while sitting in the lobby offset the frustration of waiting and confirmed my desire to work in the setting. I had the opportunity to talk with many of the older adult clients as they passed, and their warmth and friendliness made the waiting worthwhile. Your red flags and deal-breakers will be different and unique to your life and circumstances.

Deal-Breakers

Think about what you hope for in your first (or next) job. What are deal-breakers for you? Write them down.

Consider things like commute, schedule, pay, setting, etc.

Exploring these deal-breakers will help you as you job search, give you more information for the interview process, and can guide the questions you ask.

My deal-breakers: . . . .

. . . .

. . . .

. . . .

. . . .

An ideal job?

When asked to describe the ideal first job for a dance movement therapist, Hadas Weissberg said, "Wow, I have it in mind—you always dream about it! And I'm actually starting to think about it more now." She described a room large enough to move in, with a couch for when clients want to sit. She wanted it to be her own room, not a shared space, so that some of the tools she uses in her practice could be ready for use as needed. She said the most important thing was to have the space be ready for movement at any time. We joked about how much furniture-moving we creative arts therapists often do.

Sometimes in order to get the ideal space, we have to move furniture. Remember that furniture-moving is not about your aesthetic preferences—you are advocating for proper accommodations for your clients, protecting their safety and therapeutic space (Partridge, 2019c).

All joking aside, if moving furniture puts you at risk, ask for assistance. I have found it helpful to ask for and keep on file diagrams and floor plans of the rooms I work in. I can write and draw the desired placement of furniture on these diagrams to ensure clear communication with staff who help me with room setup—it decreases the likelihood of arriving to facilitate a group and needing to rearrange the room before we begin.

Donna Newman-Bluestein recommended setting aside the notion that there could be a perfect job, and instead going into your imagination and then thinking of how you might get there:

> I would have them envision. Because there isn't such a thing as a perfect job for every creative arts therapist. So I would ask them: Do you have an image of what it would be? Who it would be with? Do you have an image of how you would feel doing the work? And do you have a first step?

This idea of a first step might lead you to a particular client population, setting, or scope of work.

When thinking about what a new professional needs, Christine Hirabayashi reflected on her early internship experience: "You need to have a place that would offer a meaningful experience, with a professional who could teach you along the way." She emphasized that the most important aspects are to have the experience of an enriching interaction with clients, paired with an excellent supervisor. If there are no on-site supervisors for creative arts therapies, at the very least there should be someone who understands and respects the field and can bring out the new professional's strengths. She shared her own experience of not having an art therapist at her first placement, but how important it was to have a psychologist-mentor there who saw and celebrated her strengths.

Christine Hirabayashi and I talked about which aspects of a first job are must-haves. We agreed that the support is the most important thing: "It is about the experience. Even if it was a treatment center with a ton of money, it still wouldn't be the same if you didn't have that basis for support." I reflected back on how well-stocked and resourced the art rooms were at my first two jobs in art therapy—one in a children's hospital and the other a state hospital for sex offenders. In both cases, the well-funded art therapy program supported the work I did with clients, but the most valuable part was the excellent individual and group supervision I had and the access both places provided to additional training opportunities and professional development.

Ideal Work Environment

Do some brainstorming writing about what you would want in an ideal work environment. This exercise can help you advocate for yourself and your clients in the future.

As you write, consider what your day, week, month, and year would be like.

Write about what you would experience with all five senses.

Think about the physical space, the people you will work alongside, and the support provided by the employer, as applicable.

My ideal work environment: . . . .

. . . .

. . . .

. . . .

When she returned to Kuwait from the United States after completing her degree in drama therapy, Fatmah Al-Qadfan said she started knocking on doors of therapy centers and public schools: "Most people were interested, but hesitant. They'd say, 'Okay, we can hire you, but what else can you do if it doesn't work out?'" She said she knew that if they gave her the chance, she would probably end up with more clients than she could handle on her own. Ultimately, none of the places she first contacted were quite what she had in mind, so she began to build something of her own design: "I had a couple of kids I would see who were on the autism spectrum, and I would go to their homes and work with them, doing behavioral work and creative expression." When she started seeing adults in her practice, she decided that she needed to find somewhere to house her practice, to give her clients "the sanctity of a creative space" as well as a space that would ground her. So she reached out to the director of a clinic:

> I made an appointment, went over with my CV, and said, "This is why you should hire me: there's a need, I'm going to get clients, this is what drama therapy looks like, I can work with kids and adults." I think he was intrigued, so he checked out my credentials and saw it was a legit profession.

After having different people in the clinic meet with her, he made the decision to hire her. She said at first she was paid only for the time she saw clients, and within the first month they wanted her full-time— exactly the outcome she had predicted when she first started knocking on doors.

No matter what, you will learn from the experiences you have in your first professional roles. In describing her early work with children with medical diagnoses and then youth who had committed violent crimes, Donna Newman-Bluestein said that it was "heavy-duty" but she did it to show up as a creative arts therapist: "I just brought myself to each place and I learned whatever I could." She described both learning from the experience—what worked and what did not—and also learning directly from the clients themselves. You will learn a great deal in your early jobs post-graduation and it may feel especially tiring at first! When you are first learning to be a clinician, you have to find ways to create balance. Donna Newman-Bluestein talked about the advice she gives her students:

> I've found that when my students tell me that when they come out of a group and they're exhausted, I tell them they're doing too much of the work. What we need to see is that it is not entirely dependent on us as individuals. I don't really think that I'm a healer; I'm a person who devotes my life to healing and through which healing comes at times. But only if I make myself open; I see myself as a vessel. But I have to keep burnishing the vessel.

You should strive to leave groups energized by the work of the clients—the progress they make, the new connections they explore—rather than depleted because you have been working so hard to do the work of therapy for them. Donna Newman-Bluestein recommended keeping our expectations low, by which she meant that her expectations are not tied to huge therapeutic gains in each session but rather "to enter the space and meet the clients and have them meet me." She emphasized the need to be appreciative of the clients for showing up to do the work of therapy.

Population preferences

Creative arts therapists work with people across the entire life and health spans in a wide range of settings. Examining the *why* behind your desire to work with specific populations is essential—your own lived experience of cancer or anxiety can assist you in understanding and empathizing with clients with similar diagnoses; however, left unexamined it may be a clinical liability. Engaging in self-inquiry as to why you want to work with a population and what strengths or vulnerable spots you bring to the work is important.

Graphic medicine

The graphic medicine movement provides some potential outlets for exploration and self-inquiry. The term "graphic medicine" refers to comics and graphic novels covering topics related to providing or receiving medical or mental health care. Graphic medicine content can accomplish many different objectives including "reflecting or changing cultural perceptions of medicine, relating the subjective patient/carer/ provider experience, [and] enabling discussion of difficult subjects" (Williams, 2019), as well as giving support to providers and patients. This style of storytelling and sharing is a means to center the voices of those who are not usually heard from (Køhlert, 2019) and to more effectively communicate important information (Waite, 2019).

The emphasis on first-person narrative makes storytelling through comics particularly well suited to self-inquiry and therapist-response art. In his memoir *The Bad Doctor*, Williams (2015) explores his history with obsessive compulsive disorder along with his frustrations with the realities of medical practice. Graphic novels can also explore and expose the inner workings of care provision and therapy; Williams explored the places where personal and professional experience and struggle overlap. The ability for graphic novels and comics to communicate multilayered lived experience, a "fuller expression of multimodality" (Køhlert, 2019, p. 15), enables us to express complex human life. In *Couch Fiction*, Perry (2010) illustrated a client's progress in therapy with footnotes to explain the therapist's behavior or to give more details about the client's diagnoses and experiences.

The honesty and authenticity in works of graphic medicine can serve as a point of inspiration for you to explore your own experiences in medical and mental health care. Additionally, graphic novels about medical and mental health concerns make excellent additions to any creative arts therapist's library; some suggestions to start your collection are listed in Appendix 3. Comics can "teach us how to see the world in new and different ways" (Køhlert, 2019, p. 19). Comics and graphic novels can also help us get some insight into what different settings are like; for example, *Wrinkles* (Roca, 2016) does an excellent job of depicting the social setting of assisted living—the characters deal with fears about memory loss and navigate complex social situations.

📖 Graphic Medicine Search

After checking out the examples in Appendix 3, look for graphic medicine and other comics resources related to work you are interested in.

Do a library or web search for "graphic novel" + a population or clinical concern you are interested in working with.

Hint: Look for both print and web comics.

Therapists' histories and lived experiences

My work with people in hospital settings or receiving medical treatment has necessitated my engaging in self-inquiry around my own health care experiences (Figure 3.1).

Figure 3.1 This four-panel comic, created with graphite and ink on paper explores the different roles or stages of being a therapist with a complex health history. The text is the same in the first and fourth panels, representing the evolving awareness that a lived experience is not necessarily a liability

I have several health conditions I have had to monitor and treat since early childhood. At one point, my entire identity was as a patient. Acknowledging that some of my empathy for clients in medical care comes from my own experiences (both positive and negative) in receiving health-care services has been an essential part of my work and development as an effective, ethical therapist. This need to self-reflect is particularly important when I work with children or in psychiatric settings, where decreased social inhibitions lead my clients to ask about my medical alert bracelet or bandages from blood-draws.

One useful way my history of medical care shows up is a passion for elevating the voices of people disenfranchised by the medical setting. My own experience of being labeled and silenced makes me keenly aware of ways clients' voices are not heard. It informs both my clinical practice as well as my research methodologies; I emphasize participatory and co-research models. My history shows up in a less functional way through an attachment to the badges, keys, and having freedom of movement in medical settings. The first time I worked in a large hospital, I noticed that I felt a little surge of power when I received my badge and keys. It was such an interesting reaction I discussed it in group supervision. Bringing up my reaction along with transparency about my lived experience stimulated a powerful conversation. It enabled us to have a larger discussion about the power differentials in our setting. Left unexamined, this feeling of power may have impacted my interactions with clients.

There are many things that may have inspired your own desire to be a creative arts therapist and you should spend some time examining them. Donna Newman-Bluestein spoke about some of what draws people to become therapists—the need to be needed. Rather than viewing this need as pathological, she framed it as an opportunity to experience gratitude: "When someone is able to receive, I am grateful and I also receive."

Comic Self-Inquiry

Create a multi-panel comic about the population you want to work with. Explore characteristics you have that make you well suited to work with this population. What characteristics do you have that may cause difficulty in working with this population?

If you are currently working, explore the characteristics you bring to the work you do—where did these characteristics originate?

Breadth of experience

Though you may have an identified population you want to work with from the beginning, Christine Hirabayashi has suggested seeking a breadth of experiences over your career. Many of the contributors to this book echoed this recommendation in different ways; Donna Newman-Bluestein described how her philosophy of prioritizing doing the work of dance therapy rather than working with a specific population influenced her early career:

> I did not say "this is who I want to work with" and then follow that. I just said "I want to do the work" and then wherever that took me. So I worked with a number of different populations to start with.

Fahad al Fahed echoed some of the suggestions from Chapter 1 and the theories of job crafting; he suggested new graduates should focus on "getting work, getting a job—being open and then trying to adapt it." Doing so benefits professional development as well as the clients and organization. It means the evolving services will be better suited to the population and location. Adapting creative arts therapies into the existing setting also creates a point of differentiation for the organization or program; it will be custom-fit to the needs and interests most relevant to those it serves.

Fatmah Al-Qadfan also identified the range of populations she worked with as an essential part of her development as a therapist:

> What really shaped me, though, was the many internship oppor-tunities that had me working with various populations, from children in elementary and middle schools to folks with a range of abilities and of different ages, from clinical settings to community settings.

Experience with a wide range of clients across different settings gives you more tools to use with your clients throughout your career. For example, if you work in an acute psychiatric hospital but have experience in step-down or community settings, you better understand the resources that will be available to your clients as they leave the acute setting. You will be able to use that information to work with your client and also advocate for their needs with other providers. One of the participants in Nolan's (2019) study about community art therapy studios noted that his work in the community studio informed and was informed by his work in an inpatient program: "working within the community art therapy studio reinforced his philosophy of the importance of helping people in the inpatient setting be better equipped to function in the community art therapy studio after inpatient treatment" (p. 83). If you are not able to work in each level of care your clients will move through, you can inquire about visiting or observing.

Un-labeling

You also need to engage in a critical re-evaluation of how you label and refer to the groups of people you work with and the entire idea of "populations"—a term Gipson (2019) spelled out as often meaning people "faced with poverty, violence, and mental illness" (p. 116). You need to be careful that a desire to be of service does not interrupt listening to the individuals and communities you work with, especially if you are entering those spaces as an outsider. In her lecture at the Wellcome Trust, the poet Fiona Sampson (2016) spoke about the role of the arts in care-providing contexts and reminded attendees of the problematic history in institutional settings. She spoke about the dignity of those who receive care as an intrinsic trait: "'Dignity' names the fact that what we do to support people in health and social care is the outcome of what they are: not of what 'nice' people we might be" (para. 15).

You shape your path

The first few jobs of your career will be filled with opportunities to learn and grow. They might not be perfect. Most importantly, remind yourself you have power to shape your professional circumstances. Find ways to learn as much as possible from whatever job you are in, and do the work to continue to refine what it is that you want from your career and your work environment. The more you know yourself and what you need to thrive, the better you'll be able to find and develop those circumstances.

Pay close attention to circumstances that feel productive, growth-oriented, and fulfilling, and point your career in that direction. Pay attention to the things that feel depleting or incongruous with your ambitions, goals, and values. These will help you in making future choices about employment.

CHAPTER 4

Enlarging Your Role

Once you get a job or develop your practice, how do you push onward and upward from where you start? This chapter covers work to expand, shape, and develop individual roles for creative arts therapists. It includes program development, leadership, and creating opportunities for others in the setting. It also discusses seeking grant funding and donor support for program expansion. There can be a great deal of fear around this issue—fear about stepping into a role you are not ready for and fear about missed opportunities if you do not. You also might make choices dictated by finances rather than professional calling or interest. This chapter will help you think through the process of intentional growth and self-advocacy.

A note on finances

I have given several workshops and presentations on this idea of expanding our roles beyond those that creative arts therapists are traditionally assigned to, stretching job descriptions or taking on new and different responsibilities (Partridge, 2017, 2019b, 2019g). Each time I do so, I feel a bit conflicted, as circumstances in my family life and educational background have enabled me to make certain choices. I have had the ability to pursue things that, at least at first, run counter to a capitalistic, advancement-oriented career move. I have had the luxury to prioritize my interests over paychecks.

I think many are socialized to not talk about money or compensation, which leads to shame or discomfort in speaking up or seeking guidance about career choices. I took a big pay cut when I left a post at a state forensic hospital to work at a small nonprofit. But this choice opened up so many new doors for me. Leaving a large, regimented system (where my path to advancement was only up through the predetermined ranks) for a small organization where I could grow and evolve was the best possible choice. I acknowledge that the privilege I have and the circumstances of my life enabled this decision—I am open about discussing this fact when I speak with students or new professionals. When giving or seeking advice or guidance, you need to consider context. Curtis (2012) wrote about her lived experiences and the need to examine how her different experiences of privilege and discrimination informed her work as a music therapist. Advice is not one-size-fits-all, especially in such a highly variable and creative field.

Privilege, Support, and Barriers

Think about what privileges and supports you have had across your life.

Think about the personal and systemic barriers you have faced.

How do these two opposing forces influence your confidence in and knowledge about self-advocacy in the workplace?

Vocational awe

Vocational awe, first discussed in the context of libraries and librarianship, is relevant to the work of the creative arts therapies. Coined by Ettarh (2017, 2018) the term critiques the attitudes, behaviors, systems, and structures that perpetuate the narrative of the library as an idealized space, and sees those who work there through the lens of passion. The early writing on vocational awe makes the case for some of the difficult conversations this chapter will explore around compensation and scope of work:

> It is the people who do the work. And we need to treat these people well. You can't eat on passion. You can't pay rent on passion. It is not a sustainable source of income, and we need to stop treating vocational awe as the only way. (pandaduh, 2017)

We did not have the term for it at the time, but some of the reactions I described exploring in supervision about badges and keys in a large hospital in Chapter 3 may have been related to this idea of vocational awe—attachment to the idea of the role of the therapist or the hospital employee without interrogating the unspoken power dynamics. This emerging area of critical awareness may be very relevant not only in your workplace, but also within creative arts therapy training programs, professional organizations, and groups. Instead of viewing the work of creative arts therapy with vocational awe, which endangers both your clients and yourself, you can critique problematic histories, advocate for fair compensation, and build a sustainable career.

Building from scratch

My first job at the nonprofit was in a continuing-care retirement community; and when I started, I had a little box of art supplies and no formal scheduled groups. In the first year, I upgraded to a cart filled with supplies and my own tiny office, but I was not done growing our program. Developing the studio was a long process. It involved claiming ownership over a space and a great deal of personal and professional advocacy. When I learned that the bright pink room with windows looking out onto the courtyard had been an art studio many years prior, I made it a mission to reclaim the space. With the support of the older adult residents, my fine-arts student intern and I organized, rearranged, and took ownership of the pink room—even painting one of the walls white so we would have a good background for a photo project. Finally, a home for all our groups and for all the supplies! Perhaps most significantly, we put a sign on the door, claiming the space as an art studio, with a group schedule and a definition of art therapy. Claiming this space required some adjustment from the older adults (Partridge, 2019c), defending our territory to people who had been accustomed to using the space as a hiding spot to eat lunch, and reconsidering who participates in art therapy and how (Partridge, 2019f). Having a room dedicated to the art therapy program was a big deal in the community; it communicated to all of us involved that our work was important.

Outside the chain of command

As I grew and developed, I had several opportunities to take on larger projects. We did collaborations between our assisted-living communities, connected with community organizations, and spearheaded a nationally exhibited art show (Partridge, 2019c). Each of these opportunities enabled me to stretch and shape my role into something much larger than the job description I originally applied under. It also demonstrated value in a different way to the leadership of our organization. While personally satisfying, this collaborative work was well outside my job description as written, and sometimes resulted in role confusion or disruption of the existing reporting structure. Some of my immediate supervisors took issue with leadership above them going directly to me for implementing some of these projects. In turn, I bristled at their possessive behaviors and attempts to rein in the creative process with a hierarchical structure.

When working outside your job description, frequent, open communication is important!

Leadership change

One of the difficulties I faced was at each change or transition in leadership in my setting. Outdated ideas in the minds of people in executive director roles in particular created a challenge, requiring savvy self-advocacy to counteract their regressive ideas about what I "should" be doing. They thought I should be facilitating bingo, presiding over happy hour, and decorating for holiday parties. After a particularly upsetting interaction with a new executive director, I sat in my office trying to figure out how to help her understand the importance of the arts therapy programming in our continuing-care retirement community. I also needed to separate my personal reactions to her from my professional reactions. Our very first interchange was her admonishing me for carrying two chairs from one room to another for group, something I did many times daily: "Put those chairs down! That's a man's job," she said as she elbowed the male staff member sitting next to her. He looked at me with a panicked expression, and I made

66

a joke about being a farm girl and being used to hard work, but my joking was not well received. She often expressed displeasure about the time spent in the art studio and felt that we should spend more time decorating for every holiday and "making the residents look happy and clean." She was very concerned with the outward appearance of things rather than the deeper emotional experiences. I needed to find a way to help her see that part of meeting the care needs of the older adults was through addressing their unmet psychological and social needs—work my music therapy colleague and I were committed to.

I found that advocating for myself through the art therapy process was far more effective than trying to explain my work verbally. I asked this new executive director to tell me three words that guided her professional life. Then I invited three older adults in memory care to respond with art materials to these words to make a welcome gift for the new executive director. They created beautiful work, and in our discussion about their images, they made profound and eloquent statements about the meaning of the words in their lives and how they related them to our community. The four of us presented the three artworks in frames to the executive director one afternoon, and it was in that moment that this woman saw the importance of the work we were doing. The pride in the faces of the older adults and their ability to infuse their emotions and life stories into the images helped her see there were more important priorities than a gigantic Christmas tree in the lobby.

Transitions

The most difficult transition point for me so far was post-Ph.D. I started feeling nervous in the months leading up to defending my dissertation. I felt the increasing weight of working in a role I had outgrown and a desire to do larger things. I also had an attachment to the work and the clients I spent every day with and did not want to leave that work entirely. On the positive side, I was excited about continuing the inquiry of my dissertation research (Partridge, 2016b). I had several important conversations leading up to defending my dissertation and scheduling time to talk with our CEO. The first was with another art therapist in my doctoral program about our shared concerns about valuing our worth post-Ph.D. Hearing someone else share similar concerns helped to normalize what I was experiencing and created an opportunity to speak openly about what we were both worrying about. The second was a dinner out with my father. I invited him to a "business dinner" and asked him to help me talk through how to approach self-advocacy in the workplace. He encouraged me to consider both the financial and other benefits alongside the intellectual and other non-monetary aspects of my work. He also listened to my discomfort about openly discussing compensation and told me some stories about successful and unsuccessful requests for raises people made to him in his different management roles. This conversation with my dad helped me feel a bit more prepared and confident to talk with leadership and self-advocate.

Voicing these concerns to leadership in my organization was a bit intimidating—I was fearful that bringing up my being overqualified would lead to being fired. Having an initial conversation and following it up with a meeting with our CEO started the collaborative process of dreaming up a new role for me. We ultimately outlined an initial scope of work and focus, and the CEO determined the best team to affiliate the role with. The HR department asked me to provide guidance as to what the appropriate pay scale was for people at my experience level, as I was the first Ph.D employed in our organization. I appreciated this opportunity to be part of reimagining my role, rather than feeling forced into accepting an existing position I was not interested in or having to leave because I was overqualified and underpaid.

⌨ Important Conversations

Have a conversation with someone you work with about your hopes, dreams, and growth goals. Make a plan to check in with that person at a predetermined time in the future.

Hint: If talking with someone you work with feels too intimidating at first, consider a friend or family member.

When we made the announcement to the older adults that I would be moving into a new role, one resident offered some sage advice: "Don't let go of the sled." She explained that she had learned this saying from the native communities she worked with in rural Alaska; she cautioned me to hold on tightly to the central meaning of my work and not let momentum and excitement knock me off balance. I wrote her words on the bulletin board in my new office and still look at them frequently as I sit at my desk.

Remember this advice to hold on to the central meaning of your work as you pursue new opportunities—if you "let go" of the things that matter, you might promote into a role without any meaning to you.

Continued evolution

My role has evolved quite a bit since we first developed it. Initially, we imagined a great deal of the work would be towards developing a community of practice among our life enrichment teams, and I spent a significant portion of my first year in the role doing that. However, changing needs in our organization and opportunities to explore some exciting partnerships shifted my portfolio of work in a different direction. After being in the role for a year, we decided an alignment with the business development and strategy group was more congruous than my previous alignment with operations.

One day from my calendar demonstrates the breadth my role now encompasses:

- 6:00am: Video conference call with MIT Media Lab co-researchers to finalize our next research protocol.

- 8:45: Phone call with a fellow art therapist looking to return to work after time away to provide care for her children.

- 10:00: Meeting in the office with our HR team about the art-based findings from our recent wellness fairs.

- 11:00: Video conference call with MA student about the data analysis of her thesis research.

- 1:00: Focus group in the city where I serve on the Senior

Services Commission. I guided the participants in an art-based exploration of their vision for an age-friendly city.

- 3:30: Calendar block for reading. (As discussed in Chapter 1, I keep the last hour of my work day blocked off for reading as a way to refresh and close out my day.)

My position has grown to include service to the older adult population living in buildings my nonprofit runs, outreach and advocacy, education, attending and presenting at conferences worldwide, research, and a great deal of innovation work within our organization. I support and guide the research and other student projects—those that happen in the buildings we operate as well as those related to ideas of interest to our nonprofit. I am so grateful for the way this position has evolved, because it includes a rich diversity of work with the stability of a single, full-time, salaried job. But of course, that is not the end of the story.

Job + 1

When I began a Ph.D. program, I did not have the explicit goal of teaching. My initial focus was a desire to do research and increase awareness about art therapy with older adult populations. A need in the department and some experience as a teaching assistant led me to expand my work to include teaching in the undergraduate and graduate programs in art therapy. I fell in love with teaching and currently teach the thesis research classes, a class about aging and older adults, a class about domestic violence, and a class on the use of new media in art therapy in the VR lab. Doing this work enables a greater degree of contact with students; I love the opportunity to instill in them a love for the art in art therapy and to encourage creative practices in their thesis research.

 If you have the time and energy, what +1 would you add to your roles and responsibilities? Is there a type of work you would like to explore that is outside the role you currently have or hope to have in the future?

Growth takes time

This process of building from scratch does not happen overnight. Denise Wolf described the path to her current role today, in and out of many different settings and contexts:

> My personal career path has been really circuitous, like most of us would say. My undergrad was in art education, psychology, and philosophy. I kind of always knew that art therapy was where I wanted to go, and I knew I wanted to work in school-based settings. That was my thing—I was going to be a school art therapist. And... I'm not! I did that for a little bit as an internship and I still have a passion for school-based work: I do consulting for a large charter school and I'm providing supervision for all their school-based social workers. I saw myself doing school-based services and I kind of have come around, being the assistant director of Cedar Crest College (Allentown, PA), it is education in a different way. I have my special education certification and I'm using all of that theory to think about art therapy education. I worked for a little over 15 years in a residential treatment facility for at-risk youth. What else did I do? So many things!

Denise Wolf also identified her role as an educator as an important partner to her clinical work and vice versa: "I keep my practice because I don't want to be that curmudgeon professor who says, 'back in my day...', and I like the way teaching informs my practice and my practice informs my teaching." She described the importance of providing current, real-world examples in her classes and the infusion of contemporary literature on her private practice. She spoke about the impact she has as both a clinician and an educator—reaching and supporting communities through her own work and the work her students eventually do in the world.

Other contributors had experiences of building something from scratch in a different country than they studied in. Fatmah Al-Qadfan spoke about how she spread the word about drama therapy prior to completing her degree and returning home to Kuwait:

I knew there was no job opening for a drama therapist—I knew that going into it—that there was no job and I was going to create something. Previously, on every single vacation back to Kuwait I offered workshops at various locations. So I had collaborated with a diabetes institute, several arts and culture hubs, and dance and movement schools. I would just show up to these places, talk about my ideas, and ask if I could use their space, and they would advertise the workshop.

She described this strategy as both a great way to make a little money during graduate school and also a way to advocate for drama therapy. During this time, she was careful to connect them to local therapy resources as needed. Overall, it was a successful strategy and one she would recommend to others: "It was a great way to get people ready to meet me and my profession in a few years."

Helping something grow

When speaking about her path to advancement, Kari Rogenski explained that she first met the owner and founder of the program she works for while in a different job—they shared a client and would check in regularly about that client. She happened to mention in passing that she had an aspect of her program she was interested in expanding, and that Kari should contact her if she was interested in being involved. They reconnected later, and Kari immediately saw an opening to create space for creative arts therapies: "When I came on board, it became clear to me that if this program was going to grow and be successful it needed to be creative arts therapy-driven."

The work required balancing both the therapeutic and clinical approaches as well as the community arts lens; she described wanting to create "a program that made space for all of the above." Today, the program she oversees employs creative arts therapists, recreation therapists, teaching artists, community artists, and specialists. She described the interdisciplinarity of the program as essential in order to meet the needs of the aging population for one-on-one interaction—the "engagement and enrichment need" identified by their family members, medical providers, and case managers. The program addresses a gap in the market—people who are not interested in or otherwise connected to group or large community-based programming and would benefit from a holistic, person-centered care philosophy.

Kari Rogenski guided a growth process for the program she works for. The program started with one person, Kari, providing one-to-one creative programming for their existing care management clients. After establishing the practices of that work and hiring more staff, they began taking referrals to outside clients from other professionals in their network, and then as they grew more, taking referrals from anyone, including families. During this time, the geographical areas they served grew, from a single area to several counties in two states. As she described helping to build this program, Kari Rogenski spoke about all the things she had to learn in the process, reflecting back on her early career:

> It also was very clear to me, because I have a lot of interests and daydreams of starting my own program or my own business, but it was apparent to me at the time that I didn't know anything about business. I really didn't know anything about the market as a whole; I had no idea what it would mean to employ people—the cost associated with that. And then I had this beloved mentor who wanted to work collaboratively and who I had a shared clinical interest in working with and also a shared passion.

She attributed the successful growth of the program to these shared interests and the collaborative mentorship she has received. Her advice for other people looking to build and develop new programs is to not do it alone: "Partner with someone you truly know and truly trust. It's really hard and things get really tricky, so partner with someone who you believe in, and they believe in you. Without that it doesn't work." Growing the Hummingbird Program under the umbrella of a larger organization allowed her to create a dynamic, flourishing program in a way she says she could not have done alone: "I could have never, ever in my wildest dreams done this on my own." As you think about career goals you have and things you want to develop, keep Kari Rogenski's advice in mind.

Think about your goals for your career and what gaps you have in your skills and knowledge—these are not weaknesses, but rather opportunities for collaboration and partnership! Consider partnering with someone with a strong business or marketing background or ties to an allied field you intend to interface with.

As you think about how you want to grow, your creative practices and your dreams can help you. Dance therapist Donna Newman-Bluestein suggested tuning into your dreams as a means of exploration: "Be curious about and cultivate a relationship with your unconscious. Keep a notebook by your bed, and write your dreams when awakening."

Dreaming Your Way into New Things

If you remember your dreams and are able to take Donna Newman-Bluestein's advice to write them down upon waking up, do some response writing to the symbols or themes you see in your dreams. If you do not remember your dreams, or they seem unrelated to your professional life, begin by writing down some career and professional aspirations you have. Try not to censor yourself—put it all down on paper:

. . . .

. . . .

. . . .

. . . .

. . . .

. . . .

Once you've created this list, go back with a different color pen or pencil and circle words that stand out to you. Were there any words, phrases, or ideas that surprised you? Is there a dream that feels most familiar? As you continue to develop your path in the creative arts therapies, how might these dreams guide you?

Funding and planning

All these dreams also require funding—and there are many strategies for seeking out and obtaining grant funding. Something to consider when looking for funding is weighing the cost/benefit analysis of applying for different grants. Be sure to value your own time; see if the application requirements and then documentation requirements after being funded end up "costing" you more than they award. Sometimes the amount of the award is less than the time value it will take you to obtain and document the grant. Conversely, sometimes a small grant with a great deal of documentation requirements can lead to other opportunities.

 Explore a wide range of funding opportunities–how might small project or materials grants better support your funding goals?

Can you collaborate with someone in the interest of doing something larger than either of you might be able to do alone?

Applying for funding often means coping with rejection. Though it can feel difficult or embarrassing, follow up with the granting organization if possible. Ask about what you might do in the future for a stronger application. Watch for the award announcements and see what you can learn from the projects that were funded. It could be that you learn how to have a stronger application next year or that the foundation is not a good fit for your ideas. There is a great deal to learn from rejection, if you are willing to look and ask. You can read more about responding to rejection in Chapter 10.

Dreams also require planning. When discussing his dream to create a graduate program for art therapy at the university where he currently teaches, Fahad al Fahed identified some of his concerns:

> Because I'm teaching in arts education, I don't want to make a lot of confusion for people. Is it mental health? Is it art? What is it? So I want it to be clear from the beginning that it is a mental health profession.

For clarity's sake, he wants to develop a program as its own freestanding thing or housed within the psychology department. He created an image to explore his ideas about art therapy's future in Saudi Arabia (Figure 4.1).

Figure 4.1 "It is a mindfulness process about myself and art therapy in Saudi Arabia. On the road, focusing on the most important aspects in art therapy like education, methodology, and scope of practice for art therapists. The view is beautiful and the light is shiny, but in the early stage the need is for more qualified art therapists and more Arabic art therapy resources"

You may face similar challenges with bringing your work somewhere new. In a hospital, do you align yourself with the medical providers or with activities or recreation? Is there a mental health team and do you fit there? Mapping out allies, co-conspirators, and allegiances can assist you in this process.

Allies, Co-conspirators, and Allegiances _____

Who are your allies in your workplace?

Are there additional relationships you could nurture?

Who do you share goals with?

Do not forget to think about people outside your department, like those in HR or other areas of influence.

Most importantly, as Fatmah Al-Qadfan described, you need to remind yourself that your identity as a creative arts therapist is relevant no matter what the work looks like on the outside:

> The reality is you are going to be a therapist in a school or in a hospital or you may be helping translate or who knows, but you're still a therapist at your core. And I have to keep reminding myself of that. If I'm doing a session that appears like counseling, I'm still thinking about it as a drama therapist. My client may choose to just express verbally, but that doesn't negate the modality that I was trained in.

 "There's no one way to do our jobs."–Fatmah Al-Qadfan

You bring your identity as a creative arts therapist to every role you hold. You might start out in a role with little space for practicing the modality you studied in its purest academic form; knowing that work is inside you can help you to have patience and to have a foundation to advocate for an expanded role.

Climbing the ladder

Transitioning into leadership or supervisory roles often comes with financial and career benefits. It can enable you to influence policies, practices, and philosophies. However, knowing yourself well enough to determine if it is a good role for you is important. Donna Newman-Bluestone knew that she did not want to be an administrator in the large institutions she worked for:

> I have no interest in being the head of the department: I wanted to do the clinical work in a place where I had support and where I could support others. So after four or five years, I'd reach the end of my growth and what I could learn, and then I would move on.

Similarly, Christine Hirabayashi sought different paths to advancement instead of management, because she observed the shrinking amount of time for the direct therapeutic work for people in those roles.

◎ Boss Biases Exercise

Explore what comes to mind when you think of or hear the word "boss." You might decide to explore this in movement or sound. Or you could create an image.

When you've completed your creative exploration, write a short summary description of it.

What words do you associate with the role of the "boss" or the leader?

How might these assumptions and biases impact your decision about "climbing the ladder" at work?

In contrast, some creative arts therapists thrive in leadership roles and seek them out. Andra Duncan found great fulfillment in the teaching and advisory tasks she was responsible for once she moved into leadership. She loved the added challenge of strategic thinking and serving as a mentor. One consideration to be aware of is that being in a leadership role comes with new roles and responsibilities that may extend beyond the hourly work-week you are used to. Kari Rogenski described her experience while developing and building a program revolving around her passion for work with older adults:

The pure passion to do the work—it never goes away. It's never *not* on my mind, ever. And everything in my life right now revolves around how to help it grow and how to make it bigger and better, and how to support my staff so they can bring the magic to their clients.

Just as you need to seek balance in your roles as a creative arts therapist, you also need balance in leadership roles. If you decide taking a leap into leadership is the path for you, consider how your self-care and work-boundary practices will need to shift.

 Moving Up _____

When you think about "climbing the ladder" at work, what comes to mind?

Are you able to picture a clear path to advancement for yourself?

Do you have role models whose leadership you admire?

Imagine looking to the right and left of this ladder as well—perhaps there is a different role you are interested in pursuing.

Growing your role and scope of work may mean traditional ladder climbing, but it might also mean a lateral move or efforts to create a more creative place for yourself. Take time throughout your career to consider what it is you really want—for some people, the idea of advancement necessarily involves climbing the ladder or advancing within a set hierarchy, while others have no interest in becoming "the boss." As with everything, this interest or desire is tied to context—leadership opportunities may look far more appealing within one organization where you work than in another.

CHAPTER 5

Creative Arts Therapies Ambassadors

This chapter covers advocacy for the field—including advocating for the expansion of your own program, media outreach, interdisciplinary conversations, and other ways you can speak up and speak out. It also covers presentation strategies and experiences. Part of your ongoing professional development should include strategies for advocacy—not just for yourself but for the creative arts therapy field as a whole. The better you are at talking about the work you do, the more doors will open for you. Encountering dismissive, uninformed comments is difficult. Getting practiced at clear response and gently educating without getting defensive helps to make your field increasingly well known.

 How do people react when you tell them your profession or what you hope to study?

How do you respond?

How would you like to respond in the future?

Your first chance for advocacy is often with your own friends, family, and social networks. Donna Newman-Bluestein described having to defend her career choices while in graduate school:

> At the end of my first year of a master's program, I had the typical questions from my parents: "Well, okay, but what are you going

to do with this degree?" Particularly after I had gotten a degree in English and couldn't find a job, what made me think I could get a job as a dance therapist, something nobody ever heard of? My response was, "If there's one job out there, I'm going to get it." So again, I didn't look back. I thought, I can't allow the possibility of not getting a job.

Her perseverance and openness led her into a wide range of opportunities across her career. Your families and communities can be surrogate ambassadors of your work. Give them the tools they need by ensuring they are speaking accurately about your work and have some local resources to recommend. Your grandmother or neighbor can double your reach by speaking about your work in general.

Context matters

While describing his efforts to spread information about art therapy to people in Saudi Arabia, Fahad al Fahed said he tailors his responses to the audience. When talking to those in mental health, he draws connections between psychological theories and the work of art therapy. When speaking with people in arts education, including his students, he focuses on education and raising awareness. Smiling, he described his way to educate about art therapy with those completely outside of adjacent fields: "I try to use examples and make it relevant to their world." His approach follows the recommendations Carolan (2001) wrote about when talking about research. Fatmah Al-Qadfan also adjusts her way of speaking about drama therapy depending on who she is talking to:

I hate saying we need to legitimize our profession, but we are creative and sometimes your pitch has to change according to your audience. That's not necessarily about making our profession sound more legit: it is being emotionally intelligent and knowing our audience and our clients.

The words may change, but the core meaning stays the same. Acknowledging context is important—when addressing audiences outside our field whom I want to influence to hire creative arts therapists, I offer a range of recommendations. While my goal is always to influence people to hire creative arts therapists into full-time positions, I give a progressive hierarchy of alternatives in order to meet organizations where they are (Figure 5.1).

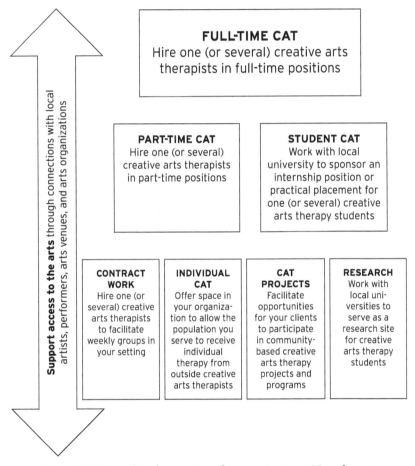

Figure 5.1 Hierarchy of suggestions for organizations. Note that arts access transcends all levels of the hierarchy, in order to promote any and all opportunities for client populations to gain access to the arts

I discuss this range when presenting in non-clinical settings—where they see and hear about the work I have been building for years and want to achieve the same results by hiring someone to come in once a month to "do a project." I gently help them adjust their expectations while advocating for peers. Another common reaction is balking at the realities of hiring a full-time creative arts therapy professional. I explain that they will gain so much in hiring a creative arts therapist—I give examples of other ways my work has impacted the organization beyond the group or individual services I provide. I always end by offering advice and guidance where possible to keep the organization and clients safe and keep the door open for them employing a creative arts therapist in the future.

Christine Hirabayashi identified some similar situations, where she was asked to train non-arts therapists to facilitate a teen empowerment program or was seen as an art teacher in a medical setting. She used it as an opportunity to educate about the field "in a gentle way" as she explains about what art therapy is, how it benefits clients, and what her background is.

Andra Duncan spoke about some of the difficulties you may face, especially when you are a new professional and still developing your sense of personal professional identity:

> We are very protective of what we do. And very protective of what it is that others do and what they can call it. As I grew professionally and more confident in myself being less worried about someone taking away what I did and making me less valuable, it only made me more valuable because I was able to share the experience of music therapy.

She spoke about educating in the workplace both about her training and scope of practice and also about the benefits of music more generally. In addition, Kari Rogenski spoke about developing a sense of confidence as your career evolves, which will enable you to better communicate what you do:

> What is drama therapy? We have the organizational definition, we have the theoretical definitions, we have the skills. But my personal experience is constantly shifting, but I'm okay with that, because I have the confidence. I'm secure enough in my identity to be okay with that.

Denise Wolf echoed this idea, describing her early-career focus on the clinical side of her work as an art therapist and on the words and labels used to describe her practice. As she developed her professional identity, she too became more confident. She felt confident in her skills and the quality of her work and less concerned with the words and labels used to describe it. This work takes time; Fatmah Al-Qadfan described giving workshops on drama therapy to medical providers and medical students as a long process of raising awareness and education:

> I've been there almost three years and now almost everyone gets what I do. We speak the same language; I'm just a lot more embodied than everyone else. At first, I felt like I was always translating into their language. I was doing a lot of explaining. Now, either my confidence has gone up or they're starting to get it. So I don't spend so much time justifying my modalities or the reason I'm doing "empty chair" or "role reversal" with a client.

In addition to advocacy inside your workplace or field, you may encounter opportunities to speak about your work on a larger platform through contact with media. Consider it an opportunity to advocate on a much larger stage.

Media Tactics

Talking about your work on the nightly news or in a magazine or news article is a bigger platform, but comes with some risks.

A few tips:

- Have the agreed upon definition from your field's professional organization or a definition from a published leader in your discipline at your fingertips.

- Send a list of preferred terms (especially if you will be speaking about a group that faces stigma) to the reporter or coordinator ahead of time.

- Try to get a sense for the angle the journalist is approaching the story with—this will help you shape your responses and enable you to guard against misrepresentation.

- Suggest some local resources or a follow-up step for the consumers of the media.

Advocating for peers

As you develop networks and spread awareness about your creative arts therapy discipline, you can create space for other creative arts therapists who come after you. Moving into a researcher role in the support center of our nonprofit gave me the opportunity to advocate for hiring more art therapists in our organization. In conversation with our vice president of business development and strategy, I explored the costs and benefits of transitioning all the roles in our life enrichment departments into creative arts therapy roles. This involved some difficult discussions around what would happen with existing staff members. In preparation for this conversation, I outlined three paths to change with estimated costs and rationales behind each. Here is where I had to practice patience—encouraged to pursue the most aggressive proposal, I fell in love with the plan. Imagining a future with dynamic, interdisciplinary departments of creative arts therapy in each community made me very excited. However, change often comes slower than I would like. Several years later and we have budding internship programs in two buildings for creative arts therapists and several additional creative arts therapy staff, but not the complete reimagining we discussed in those meetings. Staying committed to a change process is difficult when the change happens slowly. Finding ways to reinvigorate the discussion can help.

This role has allowed me to define best practices and make recommendations for our communities. I also worked with existing staff to safely and ethically integrate creative practices into the work we do, acknowledging the different levels of training. Building a team of people who believe in the importance of creativity in all our programming supports the work of the creative arts therapists we employ; I created a graphic and info sheet to assist in training and teaching about creativity in our context (Appendix 2). This process has not always gone smoothly and has had its share of frustration and heartbreak. Sometimes, I thought I had an ally or a breakthrough with someone, and then they turned around and called our work "activities" or said "bingo is fine." In the moment, these feel like crushing blows— but the experience helped me learn that advocating for the field and the work of creative arts therapists is a process.

 ## Speaking Up

How do you speak up for your creative arts therapy discipline?

How do you speak up for students and new professionals?

How do you speak up or advocate for the field as a whole?

As Andra Duncan mentioned, in your protectiveness over your work, you may stumble in your attempts to communicate. Spending some time formulating how you will talk about your role makes you a better advocate. If you feel hesitant about doing so, ask peers or mentors about what they say. Listen carefully when you hear people introduce themselves or introduce you. If there are words or labels you especially like, use those the next time you introduce yourself. If there are words you do not like or that make you uncomfortable, make note of them. In either case, explore what those words or phrases seem to be communicating. This exercise also allows you to consider ways you might integrate other aspects of your personal and professional identity into your communication.

Conferences and presentations

Regional or national conferences offer opportunities for professional development, reconnecting with former classmates and colleagues, and often opportunities to express and explore in community. The benefits of conference attendance for continuing education is covered in Chapter 8; the current section focuses on your professional role development through conference presentations and attendance.

It may feel overwhelming the first time you consider submitting a proposal to a conference—there are a few strategies to overcome this.

When attending conferences, make notes to yourself about aspects of presentations or workshops you especially enjoy. When considering a proposal, think about areas of expertise you have, interesting clinical experiences, or specific techniques you have developed. This will help you craft your proposal and presentation. Some conferences host informational sessions about writing proposals, which can be very helpful for getting questions answered and seeing what makes a successful proposal.

If you have a peer or mentor who can review your proposal prior to submission and your presentation prior to the conference (remember your academic network from Chapter 2!), that is a great help. Do not underestimate the power of presenting aloud to your pets or in front of the mirror—doing so will help you catch awkward phrasing, repeated words, or unclear parts of your talk. There are many tips and tricks for public speaking which you can utilize in preparation. When it is time to present, try to relax and enjoy it! To extend the conversation beyond the conference, you might consider creating something for your attendees to stay in contact with you or access more resources.

When it is time to give your talk, be as natural and present as possible—people attend conferences to see and hear the content come to life—so do not just read aloud from a written paper.

Do not forget to breathe while you are presenting!

Presenting about your work as part of conferences in other fields helps to spread the word about the work you do. It is also an opportunity to learn more about advocacy; preparing and delivering a professional presentation helps you hone the language you use to discuss your work and to tailor your focus to the audience. You can connect with clinicians who share specialties but diverge in approaches. You can also draw connections between your work and those operating from completely different perspectives. Denise Wolf endorsed attending and presenting at conferences related to art therapy, but also to her other interests and specialties in trauma and human trafficking.

When I attended and presented at a conference for social history curators in Scotland (Partridge, 2019e), I found so many areas of common concern and interest between their fields and art therapy. I also love attending a yearly research conference about diseases of later life with a focus on the basic science and the microcellular disease processes. Although these are not directly relevant to my day-to-day work, hearing about new discoveries and areas of interest helps me to contextualize the work I do with older adults within the larger scientific and social world.

 What conferences or topic areas are you interested in exploring?

Even if it scares you, you will gain so much from presenting. Kari Rogenski believes learning to speak about your work will impact your professional esteem: "When you have to speak about your work at a higher level, to have conversations across disciplines, that matters."

Always an advocate

You may find yourself confronted and questioned about the work you do throughout your career. It begins in school—Denise Wolf talked about being told she and her peers were pioneers in the field: "I became pretty resentful of that over time, being a pioneer. What does that mean? Because if we constantly think of ourselves as pioneers, it means that our field isn't solidified." This distinction is important: you can advocate for your work and for yourself without diminishing or dismissing the field as new, emerging, or less-than—tactics Denise Wolf described as "dangerous to convey."

Coleen Lorenz said she could not think of a time she did not have to advocate for the field. She attributed this need to the nature of the work: "Movement therapy is so raw!" Part of your job as a creative arts therapist is to advocate for your specific specialties, the creative arts therapies overall, and for creative expression in general. Donna Newman-Bluestein described advocating for the field as a "daily practice" she engages in: "Of all of the arts, dance can be the most intimidating—because we have such a mind–body split." She works to help heal this split by sharing articles and information on social media about the power and potency of the arts, and to try to influence what she described as the "upside down values" that do not prioritize the arts in our lives and value things above people. When you are talking about and advocating for the creative arts therapies, remember that your behavior and words reflect on the field as a whole. Answer questions, even if it seems like the question-asker should already know the answer.

Client or group needs are another reason you need to advocate for your creative arts therapy discipline. Hadas Weissberg brought up something she noticed in her early work: when assigned to facilitate groups, she was rarely given a big room with space for movement—"I sometimes had to meet with patients in a place where we couldn't really move…so sometimes we were working on the breathing or other things, but it was not the best." Her supervisor was not a dance movement therapist and so was not thinking about the space and logistical needs of a dance therapy session; Hadas needed to speak up and request more appropriate space. She also talked about how she advocates for the field in more casual ways—with a short elevator speech about dance movement therapy and preparation for the follow-up questions. When asked about her work, she replies, "Dance movement therapy is a psychotherapy but we are using our body and mind and the fact that they connect to each other." When people ask if they have to be a dancer or know choreography to participate, she says, "No, you just have to bring yourself and your body and to be there in the moment. And you find out how amazing this tool is." She said that people often give her feedback that when she describes it, it makes a lot of sense to them to combine movement and body with the therapeutic tools. She also described the difference in being close to a well-known training program versus being away from one: proximity to training programs may mean a more informed general public. She cautioned that you need to be aware that you will still have people comparing the work you do to other more well-known mental health roles or describing it as solely an adjunct treatment; she says she hears, "It's nice and good but not instead of traditional psychotherapy." These are great opportunities to practice your non-defensive advocacy for the field.

Service to the field

There are many opportunities to provide service to your local, regional, national, and international organizations. Kari Rogenski has been working with the North American Drama Therapy Association since she first entered the field: "I really wanted to become more involved in what it means to be a drama therapist and I really wanted to push the boundaries on what drama therapy is." She spoke about the importance of getting involved with the national organization—starting when she was a student as a volunteer at the conference and continuing till today, as current president-elect. She said this service at the national level has also contributed to her personal professional identity: "That has allowed me to really own my identity as a drama therapist in a way that has given me more confidence and power than I ever had before, even though I've been a drama therapist for many years."

Service to the field regionally or nationally can end up benefiting your personal development—you will make connections to people and organizations who may provide job leads or be collaborators in the future.

Informal presentations in the community

Speaking about the work you do in community settings offers opportunities to network, to spread awareness about the work of creative arts therapists, and to encourage creativity and self-expression. Christine Hirabayashi talked about the importance of accepting these requests wherever possible, and returning the calls or requests for information as an opportunity to "share more about the field, our national association, and a little bit about what I do and why I enjoy what I do. I think it is the responsibility of being an art therapist." She said she sees the public exhibition put on by people she works with (in an open studio for people living with chronic pain) as another way to do informal advocacy for art therapy in the community.

Donna Newman-Bluestein spoke about ways to talk about the arts in general that will benefit you when you do public talks. She suggested focusing on what the arts provide us as humans: "The arts are about finding what is meaningful and important to each of us, and the arts are about the relationship between the parts and the whole." This focus will help your general audience find "something for them" in your talk, even if the rest of it is about a clinical population or setting they do not identify with. Methods of writing and speaking suggested by the FrameWorks Institute[1] can help you come up with ways to present about your work in a way that has influence and impact.

You want to be careful not to frame your clients as "the other." Focusing on what everyone can gain from arts participation is one way to be more inclusive.

So what does this look like in practice? Thanks to a connection via a former painting professor, I was invited to present about art therapy to a group of people taking an art class at a community arts center. I gave a broad overview, shared some examples of work with a range of client populations, and concluded by talking about what we know so far about the benefits of the arts. I have given similar presentations to retirees at a program run by a university alumni association. I usually include different ways attendees might engage in the arts in their daily life. These one-time opportunities put ripple-effects of advocacy out into the community. Your goal is to inform the audience so that when they hear about your creative arts therapy discipline in the future, they know what it is and can contextualize what they are hearing.

---

1   http://frameworksinstitute.org/frameworks-celebrates-20-years-by-reaffirming-the-power-of-how.html

CHAPTER 6

Non-traditional Roles

Sometimes your career path necessitates assuming a role or identity other than the one you set out to have. This chapter covers creative arts therapists working in non-traditional roles and positions. You may get a job working in a non-clinical setting where your identity as a creative arts therapist is unknown or is less visible. I remember very clearly the first time my employee badge listed "Art Therapist" as my job title. It was far from my first art therapy job, but it was the first time my title aligned with my professional identity; as my new supervisor (a music therapist) handed me the badge, I felt tears well up in my eyes. Job titles are important; they "have meaningful implications for employees, both on and off the job" (Grant, Berg, & Cable, 2014, p. 1201). Titles are not everything though. You may be able to bring your unique qualifications and skillsets to interesting non-traditional roles or while working under less-than-ideal job titles. You can live out the practices of your vocation in an ever-expanding variety of roles; there are still assets and skills you bring from your creative arts therapy training to whatever work you are doing.

 Job Title _____

If your job title is not related to your therapeutic role, what would you want it to be?

Are there elements of this desired title you can incorporate into your official work?

_____

Self-care still matters

When in a non-traditional role, you can still use the skills of clinical work and will benefit from the self-care and self-preservation techniques you learned as well. I began using the ProQOL (Professional Quality of Life measure) (Stamm, 2009) as a self-monitoring tool while working in the forensic environment. I used it, as suggested by Stamm, as a self-administered evaluation of my "ongoing self-care plan" (p. 14). I found it useful to consider both the positive satisfaction I gained from work as well as tracking negative issues like burnout and compassion fatigue. I continued the practice when I moved to work with older adults and now in my role as a researcher. The thing that shifts is the "who" of the clients. In my researcher role, I think about the participants in my research, my collaborators, my colleagues, and my students as the "who" I am helping.

Who Are My Clients?

If your role is something other than the therapist or clinician you thought you would be or have been in the past, who are your clients?

Create an image or other form of creative expression describing the needs, characteristics, and concerns of the clients you serve in a non-traditional role.

Hint: You might want to imagine how they would describe themselves and your relationship to them. What words would they use?

Many of the contributors to this book spoke about valuing the flexibility they have through non-traditional roles. We shared laughter about the coexisting stress and joy of doing many kinds of work at once. Denise Wolf talked about the way her students react to hearing about the different work she does:

Some of my students have said to me, "Do all art therapists have nine jobs?" I think they find that both terrifying and inspiring. The question is, do I need to have nine jobs to have a sustainable career because I'm not going to make a living doing just one thing? And my answer anymore is no, but being that we are creative people, inherent in art therapist identity is that we seek out multiple opportunities to be creative. And so our jobs look like a little bit of a mess from the outside, because that's the nature of who we are.

You will need to consider how each thing you add to your list of responsibilities and roles will impact your overall life. In addition to her work running a creative arts therapy-oriented program, Kari Rogenski is also involved in organizing and leading in an interdisciplinary group promoting creative aging. This leadership role involves collaboration with other creative arts therapists, professionals in the field of aging, and teaching artists. This work can be very fulfilling, but requires attention to her role and time constraints:

> I am really learning to work collaboratively, because the leadership roles I hold in these different organizations is very different, so I've had to learn when to step up and step back. And how to have healthy boundaries around what I have the capacity to give.

You may need to engage in regular check-ins with yourself about what you contribute and where you have to say "no," and what is most important in your schedule and work life. Fatmah Al-Qadfan was reluctant to give up flexibility of a mixed portfolio of jobs for a full-time position:

> I liked doing different things. I was volunteering with the juvenile detention center; I was still working with different dance schools, doing my own workshops; and now all of a sudden they wanted me tied down to one clinic. I signed on part-time thinking I'd do a little bit of both worlds.

Demand for her services necessitated shifting again; her client caseload built up so quickly that she did end up transitioning into a full-time role, but she maintains enough flexibility to continue offering weekend workshops and doing some of the other work she enjoys, even though she has entered a more traditional role. Your self-care needs will evolve as your career does—strategies that work in one role may not be as effective when you change jobs. Be open to ways your needs and preferences will evolve along with your career.

Ethics

When in non-traditional roles, professional boundaries may be less clear-cut or perceived to be less clear at first glance. The work you do may not happen behind the closed door of a therapy office or studio, which will require you to think about how you engage in an ethical manner.

 How will you keep the people you are providing creative arts therapy for safe?

How will you uphold the principles and ethical guidelines of your profession?

When conducting arts programming in non-traditional settings, I have found it useful to speak aloud some of the language we use in informed consents—gently making people aware that we are working in a public space and that the art we do may stimulate strong emotions. Even with a warning, emotional reactions may catch participants in your programming off-guard.

One time, a leader in my organization started crying in a big leadership meeting because she had not realized how overwhelmed she was feeling until making art about her workload. Depending on the setting, it may be more or less appropriate to check in with the person individually in the moment or later. In this case, I followed up with this person after the meeting to see if there was anything she wanted to talk about or any way I could be supportive of her process with the image. She stated she was actually glad it happened, because it helped her see just how overwhelming things had become. I reassured her that it was okay to have strong reactions to the work, and that I was also glad she found it helpful.

The non-traditional therapist

Is a non-traditional role for you? Exploring how you would show up in a non-traditional role is an important first step—particularly if stepping into this role involves a significant career or personal life adjustment. You also want to think through some of the logistical and practical matters: If the non-traditional role does not require licensure, will you maintain your license and credentials? What parts of your professional self will you be putting on hold or setting aside to do this work? What new skills will you learn by taking this step? Spend some time thinking through the short- and long-term impact of the possible transition.

◎ Self-portrait Project

Create a self-portrait of yourself as a clinician and then in a non-traditional role, or create a dual portrait.

Consider how you might depict the ideal or positive features as well as the worst days.

Hint: You might want to explore using staged selfies or altered photos.

In creating my own split image, I thought about some of the fears I had prior to my transition from a strictly clinical role to my current role as a researcher. I was worried about missing the dynamic work in the assisted-living community: the fast pace of moving all over the building, the full schedule of groups, and the dynamic work I was doing with the residents. I pictured myself sitting in a dim room, with a computer, removed from the varied and fast-paced clinical world. I return to this vision when I have difficult days at my desk, or when it has been too long since I have had unstructured time with the older adults to create, or when I've received a particularly painful grant or manuscript rejection (Figure 6.1).

Making an extreme image like this one can help you see assumptions you are making or reveal erroneous binary thinking. In reflecting on this image, I realized how much variation and flexibility I actually do have in my job (including the flexibility to make the image at my desk in the first place!).

When working in a non-traditional role, to meet your desire to be in creative community with others or to feel clinically useful, you may need to find ways outside your full-time job. When I began teaching and working as a researcher, I missed having daily opportunities to do art therapy. Offering sporadic art therapy groups from my studio and seeing a few private clients gave me just the right amount of access to my identity as a clinician. I also schedule time to make art and spend time with older adults outside research sessions.

Figure 6.1 "Portrait of the Removed Researcher"—India and acrylic ink with collage on paper. I drew myself with my head in my hand, worried expression on my face, in front of the computer. The thought bubble contains collaged paper and translucent tape in multiple colors, representing my idea that clinical work is more varied and multilayered

CHAPTER 7

Non-traditional Settings

This chapter covers work in non-traditional and non-clinical settings, bringing the creative arts therapies to new areas and democratizing access to therapeutic services. There are some important things to think about when you are contemplating working in a non-traditional setting. A traditional setting may have systems set up to support the clinicians who work there, whereas in a non-traditional setting, things like supervision, continuing education, and professional development are not necessarily part of the workflow. How you work with clients changes in a non-traditional setting as well, though perhaps with more nuances than the older binary models of clinical versus community settings:

> Today the old dichotomy in art therapy seems to be resolved due to the understanding that art therapy exists across a continuum of practice that art therapists can adapt to responsively according to their clients' needs. Cocreated art therapy spaces invite integration within therapy, allowing the therapist to bridge the dichotomy between community and clinical art therapy. (Nolan, 2019, p. 77)

What matters is the work you do and how you show up to do it, not the setting itself. As Denise Wolf observed, "just because you're in a non-clinical setting doesn't mean you're not doing art therapy." She went on to talk about how past glorification of the clinical role as better than or more important "drives a wedge in the field and creates haves and have-nots and us versus them." It also creates false hierarchies among client populations—who deserves or has access to the work you do based on the setting, diagnoses of clients, or your title. Talwar (2019b) wrote about both the rewards and benefits of this work outside traditional clinical settings as well as the messy ambiguity of it.

You need to take care that your work with the "identified client" or "identified patient" does not neglect the needs and interests of those in the client's support communities. In family work, it is understood that treating individuals may involve some treatment with or processing for their families. You may be less mindful of how this same pattern of context and community erasure perpetuates across organizations. How might your practice of expressive therapy impact and support the staff and care professionals you work with or not? One of the participants in Nolan's (2019) study created an opportunity for staff to participate in an open studio as a means to take care of themselves amidst a chaotic work environment. Alternatively, stepping out of clinical work entirely, how might creative arts therapies integrate into community, workplace, or non-therapeutic settings? What are the unique challenges and triumphs of this work? Creative arts therapists are beginning to engage in more critical examination of how and where they work (Talwar, 2019a, 2019b).[1] Curtis (2012) wrote about the relationship between the context of the work and social justice in music therapy.

Needs and Benefits

Let's explore this a bit more...because there are definite benefits to traditional and clinical settings, but non-traditional settings have exciting potential too.

Traditional setting

For our clients:
What benefits and supports does a traditional setting provide to clients?

. . . .

. . . .

. . . .

What needs does a traditional setting fill?

. . . .

---

1   See also www.criticalpedagogyartstherapies.com

....

....

For therapists:
What benefits and supports does a traditional setting provide to therapists?

....

....

....

What needs does a traditional setting fill?

....

....

....

For community:
What benefits and supports does a traditional setting provide for the whole community?

....

....

....

What needs does a traditional setting fill?

....

....

....

Non-traditional setting

For our clients:
What benefits and supports does a non-traditional setting provide to clients?

....

....

....

What needs does a non-traditional setting fill?

....

....

....

For therapists:

What benefits and supports does a non-traditional setting provide to therapists?

....

....

....

What needs does a non-traditional setting fill?

....

....

....

For community:

What benefits and supports does a non-traditional setting provide for the whole community?

....

....

....

What needs does a non-traditional setting fill?

....

....

....

Take a look back at your answers to these questions and identify those that pique your interest. Likewise, identify areas of work that you feel uncomfortable with or hesitant to carry out. These questions can help you to identify passion and purpose in your work, and may help you make decisions about the types of settings you work in.

Thinking differently about how and where you do your work as a creative arts therapist can help you reach people traditional programs are not currently supporting. Kari Rogenski described how the program she works with meets the needs of individual older adults:

> We weren't interested in doing group programs. We are happy to be a support, but what we were interested in addressing was the gap in the market—the unmet need of the individual. One of the mistakes we make in elder care day programs is group programming. A lot of people are not group people—I'm not even that much of a group person! I am a great group leader, but if you ask me if I want to go to the gym and join a Zumba class or use the weight machines, I prefer to do my own thing. There are so many of us who may not be group joiners at all. That was the idea behind it. Homing in on the market objective of the one-on-one programming was essential to help it spread and grow.

 Consider how services are currently provided to a population you work with now or are interested in working with in the future. Whose needs are being met by these programs? Who might not be getting what they need from the current practices? How could you change things to meet the needs of others?

Thinking about gaps in service provision might bring up the need for difficult conversations. Kari Rogenski spoke about having sensitivity with people who feel like they are already doing the work you are suggesting; she suggested an additive approach that avoids criticizing existing practices, instead focusing on those whose needs are not currently met. She does a great deal of education about who their program supports and how it can supplement existing programs.

After considering the benefits and needs supported by non-traditional settings, you also need to examine the barriers and difficulties as well. For example, some community programs may have to make certain choices about whom the program serves as a means to ensure safety— creating an unequal level of access. Or the hours may only serve those who work traditional schedules; given the social and other health impacts of night shift workers (Harrington, 2001), you need to think about ways to intentionally create space for them. In many traditional settings, the night shift carries out the essential work of preserving safety, performing essential tasks, and saving lives.

How might non-traditional therapeutic settings be established to meet the needs of night shift workers and other people who may miss out on workplace or community support offerings?

If there are night shift workers connected to the work you do, how might you get involved in proving support?

Creative arts therapy in the workplace

Therapy can meet growing needs in many different workplace settings. Businesses are worried about how to support employees' needs beyond the paycheck; people in leadership contemplate, "with an increasingly global and remote workforce, how do we keep our teams connected and feeling like they're part of something bigger than themselves?" (The School of Life & Microsoft, n.d.).

If you currently work in a setting that employs more than a few people, consider how you might be able to support your coworkers.

Talk with your supervisor or HR department about what that support could look like.

Your dynamic, imaginative work can assist people in their own job crafting (Wrzesniewski et al., 2010; Wrzesniewski & Dutton, 2001) and workplace stress reduction.

After several years of work as an art therapist in communities providing care and services for older adults (Partridge, 2019c), I began offering opportunities for care providers to engage in creative practices. Stress in the workplace, particularly among direct care providers, is a significant concern that may benefit from arts-based interventions, and needs further study (Gillam, 2018; Huet, 2015, 2017). In the first few years in our communities, these opportunities were limited to in-service training for certified nursing assistants and registered nurses in the skilled nursing department or an occasional stress relief group for resident assistants in a memory care community. Later, we began to develop more robust opportunities for creative practices (Partridge & Jordan, 2019). These included breakroom art journals, monthly drop-in groups to make art in my office, and chalkboard walls in employee locker rooms. The early opportunities to present directives in leadership workshops were met with skepticism. Gradually, as creative and art-based practice became more of a familiar tool, and as creativity became an essential and desirable skillset upon hire, participants expressed anticipation and appreciation for time to create, as opposed to murmurs of fear or displeasure when I entered the room with boxes of art supplies.

It was surprising to me to witness the lack of basic competencies with materials—things like leaving lids off of glue when done or smashing markers against paper—behaviors I would expect from young children but not executives and managers. My entreaties to put lids and caps on securely became a running joke at leadership meetings, and I became increasingly curious about what I was observing. As a means to connect the work to other art therapy literature, I conducted a survey of leadership about comfort and familiarity with materials based on the expressive therapies continuum (Hinz, 2009; Lusebrink, 2004, 2010). I asked people to assess the appropriateness of different art materials in the workplace and to report their familiarity and comfort with each medium. This and other program evaluations of our workplace creativity projects taught me about gaps in knowledge of art material use and research methods. Repeated exposure and more simplified instruction and rationale helped with misunderstandings about program evaluation. To address the misuse of materials, I incorporated education about how to use materials into each experience.

We have also been exploring the use of creative practices to introduce new business conversations in our monthly operations meeting. As a means to introduce a new sustainability initiative, leaders were invited to give their own definitions of sustainability and to create a small art piece on a green paint chip sample-card of their choosing. The resulting images and written definitions captured nuances in our leadership team's ideas about sustainability. We have learned, as is consistent with research about facilitated versus unfacilitated arts (Kaimal et al., 2017), that opportunities for engagement work best when facilitated or when they have an on-site champion. Though I would love our staff to feel inspired to create on their own since I cannot be present in every breakroom at all times, the research and our pilot experiments suggest that facilitated creative experiences may be our best bet. We have also learned that it helps if people in leadership roles model active participation instead of just recommending that employees participate. The process seems to be working; our director of clinical services recently told me, "You've taught us we can have a conversation without words."

As we develop new ideas in our organization, we experiment with different creative ways to invite other team members into the process, stimulate dialogue, and disperse ideas. The team I belong to regularly does what we call "gallery walks" where we create visual installations to describe new ideas. We include elements that would otherwise be incorporated into a slide deck, but instead use patterned paper, collage, found objects, and vintage typographical elements to create little installations. Once set up, coworkers are invited to come into the room and walk around the table as gallery visitors. They can add thoughts, comments, and questions via sticky notes. After they have had opportunities to review everything in the room, we have a conversation. Getting away from the computer and projector invites a more embodied experience, and we have found the discussions to be far more dynamic and exciting.

These kinds of ideas are part of how you can demonstrate value in the non-traditional setting. You might consider ways to incorporate your creative practice into necessary aspects of the work environment as a way to create more interest and participation. Mandatory training or regular meetings are a great forum. In collaboration with a music therapist and the nurse-trainer, we used art and music therapy to facilitate a mandatory training about patients' rights. Incorporating singing and image-making into the mandatory yearly training transformed the staff's experiences—both of the content and their experiences of us.

Bringing art therapy to new countries

One of the non-traditional settings you might work in is when or if you bring your creative arts therapy practice somewhere new—becoming what has been termed a "sojourner" therapist (Gómez Carlier & Salom, 2012), a process the authors posit necessitates both internal and external changes on behalf of both the therapist and the profession. Fatmah Al-Qadfan and Fahad al Fahed both spoke about creating new audiences for their creative arts therapy discipline after studying in the United States. Fahad al Fahed undertook his individual practicum in his doctoral program about how to bring art therapy to new places; he did a Delphi study about what to include and what not to include in a training program for art therapists in Saudi Arabia. One point he emphasized was the need to "pay attention to what is available" and adapt art therapy to fit the new place as opposed to just importing theories and practices without connection to the existing culture and healing processes already in use in the place. Bringing a creative arts therapy practice somewhere new requires more than just translation of training materials into the local language, though that is important as well.

Acknowledging the context of your work is essential. When thinking about how to bring your creative arts therapy practice somewhere new be sure you think about what you are doing in the way of translating, adapting, or inventing.

 ## Barriers to Access
Whether you are bringing your practice somewhere new or working in an established setting, you need to think about the barriers to access to your services. Jot down some thoughts about existing or possible future barriers to accessing creative arts therapy.

Consider:

- cost (both the cost of service and all the other ancillary costs)

- stigma

- transportation

- awareness

- "Whom does my work serve?"

- "Are certain groups unable to access my services or offerings?"

For each barrier you identify, answer the question: "How can I address this barrier?"

Barriers to accessing my services:.................................

....

....

....

....

Stigma

One of the potential benefits to offering creative arts therapy services in non-traditional settings is to work around areas of stigma. Stigma can prevent some people from seeking therapy at all (Vogel et al., 2017), particularly when there are additional layers of traditions, beliefs, and practices that are different from a Western, medicalized approach to mental health services. Clients can experience different types of stigma, originating from within themselves or from others, which can impact the progress and outcome of therapy (Owen, Thomas, & Rodolfa, 2013).

Non-traditional settings may help address some of the social stigma. While travelling in Scotland, I encountered a delightful bookshop—filled with new and gently used self-help and personal development books. The storefront was also an access area to a therapy practice, which enabled people to walk into the shop with less worry about stigma—both for seeking therapy or being in the self-help section of a larger bookstore. It was a brilliant idea that should be replicated. Imagine a music therapy center with a music shop at the front or an art therapy office with a gallery or art supply store at street level!

 What do your clients encounter before their sessions and groups with you? Think about their entire journey to the start of the session.

Consider for a moment the door to accessing your services.

What the door looks like and how it is labeled can play a role in increasing or decreasing stigma. How might the building itself stimulate a greater sense of inclusion?

Advertisements, signage, and the building itself factor into a client's sense of belonging. Buildings can be considered as part of the therapeutic work: "a person's ability to be located in a place or to have a sense of belonging is fundamental to his or her wellbeing" (Smith, 2019, p. 245). Making therapy a visible, common part of people's everyday lives can help to destigmatize mental health treatment. Jess Minckley created an image in response to this idea, which she titled "Doorway" (Figure 7.1). She described the piece as being about stigma-reduction and future change:

> "Doorway" is about making advances in treatment, including stigma-reduction. This door is open to multiple possibilities. Our office doors are open to our clients to illuminate new ways of understanding themselves and their cosmos. We try to remain open-hearted. We are welcoming changes to traditional means of healing. We aim to adapt to new challenges as they arise—such as increasing accessibility for folks who may feel stigmatized by traditional mental health care. We open up discourse possibilities on behalf of others, and with the help of other practitioners. *We hold space.* We help people recreate their stories: art therapy is a place where they can reimagine what it means to heal, and the physical, temporal, phenomenological space we create impacts that transformative, imaginative process.

How will your work be part of this change Jess Minckley described?

Figure 7.1 "Doorway"—digital drawing by Jess Minckley

Arts outside therapy

Part of democratizing access to the creative arts includes creating points of access to the processes and benefits outside formal treatment or therapy settings. Sampson (2016) spoke about the ways the arts, and poetry in particular, gain access to spaces where they do not traditionally exist: "Art is many things, but above all it is additional, creative, disobedient and indirect. Poetry, that cheapest and most portable of all its forms, sneaks into the unit, on the bedside table or overheard in a dayroom" (para. 29). This access may take the form of aftercare or former-client open studio groups or groups designed for the non-clinical public. If the only access someone has to these services is as a person with a diagnosed disorder, that person may stay symptomatic or hold themselves back from recovery as a means to preserve access to valued services.

 Think about your clients—are there ways they might be worrying about continued access to the benefits and positive aspects of your services as they become more stable? What can you do to address these fears?

In her work with people with chronic pain, Christine Hirabayashi works both in a formal, structured treatment setting as well as facilitating an open studio and yearly art exhibition of open studio participants' work. She spoke about the benefits she observes from the yearly show: "The open studio provided a place to be creative, but beyond that the event, being there at the opening, gave them something to be proud of." She described one participant for whom participating in an exhibition was far outside her comfort zone. The artist had invited family to the opening and shared how seeing her work on the walls helped her family understand what she had been going through and how art therapy had helped her. Christine reflected on the mechanisms at play in the exhibition: "It is the idea of taking all their experiences and putting it in the creative piece, and hanging them together alongside their words and what they've experienced." She said she believes this exhibit helps the viewing public better understand the meaning and power of art therapy as well as the lived experience of chronic pain.

In describing the work she does at her wellness center, Coleen Lorenz said that while they do get county funding to operate some of their programs geared towards mental health and those who have been in the criminal justice system, their focus is not on diagnosis and disorder. People can bring their experiences to the setting, but they do not have to dwell in the more clinical work: "They can come in as broken as they want." Through the wellness center, she has had the opportunity to develop and grow programs for other providers—workshops in stress reduction and resilience. The more clinical, traditional part of your work can help fund work that is more or differently accessible.

Tawanna Benbow spoke about her reason for building a practice based on vacation retreats. Her Golden Thread Workshops invite participants to engage in healing the "surface wounds" sustained over a lifetime. Participants can engage in therapeutic growth work while gifting themselves time spent on a vacation. She spoke about the powerful realization participants have that they are not alone when enough people with shared surface wounds enter into a shared space. Though connection over shared experience can happen anywhere, her background enables greater access to people's emotional and spiritual needs: "With my niche and my experience I can delve a little deeper using exercises and imagery to externalize emotions and feelings...it is a broader stroke on a wider palette." These types of hybrid spaces, combining therapeutic philosophies with leisure can democratize and destigmatize access to the healing and self-understanding through the arts. One of Nolan's (2019) research participants also works in this way, working with clients seeking "opportunities for self-discovery using art" (p. 83).

When she was assisting with supporting a child actor in a large production, Fatmah Al-Qadfan said that while the other participants in the production were sometimes confused about her role and why a drama therapist was at rehearsals, they also used her presence as an opportunity to ask her questions about therapy and mental health concerns. When you interact in a hybrid space, you might be the first mental health provider someone has an opportunity to talk with.

In these non-traditional spaces, you need to define the purpose and philosophy of your work. Understanding where you are on the continuums between therapy and instructional classes, or therapy and performance or exhibition, has ethical implications. Over the course of your career, you might swing between traditional and non-traditional work; the better grasp you have on the risks and benefits of this varied work and your own professional identity (which you will explore in Chapter 8), the greater the support you can provide to your clients and communities.

CHAPTER 8

Professional Identity

Your professional identity will continue to grow and change across your career. This chapter includes strategies for developing your professional identity as a creative arts therapist. It discusses licensure from a philosophical and professional practice perspective—acknowledging that your local, regional, and national licensing and credentialing bodies are the best source for current information on these topics. It includes discussion of and philosophies about continuing education, both formal continuing education programs and independent creative and intellectual development. This chapter also presents stories about dual degrees or certifications that people have found helpful in their job outlook or career development.

When considering your work outlook, you want to balance your professional identity with your personal needs and preferences. Your training and professional identity can shape the life you lead, or vice versa. Doing some deep thinking ahead of time can enable you to take the types of bold steps Fatmah Al-Qadfan described in Chapter 3. Listen closely to the way your professors and site supervisors describe their own professional identities. What words resonate for you? How do you hope to describe yourself someday? Depending on the setting you work in and the state or region, dual licensure or additional certifications may be necessary. As discussed in Chapter 2, some consideration of licensure and credentialing should happen prior to entering a training program. One good recommendation Kari Rogenski suggested: "Save everything, and keep what you have well-organized."

Save everything. Ask questions early and often. And keep back-up records of everything you have done towards your professional identity.

Fahad al Fahed describes his professional identity by describing how he approaches his work philosophically:

> I'm more interested in personality. Understanding personality through art, through visual elements. Because I believe that most of the problems and conflicts start from the personality, I'm interested in the personality and the character of the person. I try to put these theories together—the psychoanalysis theory, the cognitive behavioral theory, the gestalt, the narrative, the positive—trying to see what is common. What they are looking for and what they are trying to provide for one person. I try to see what the integrated picture is.

His self-definition of using art therapy to see the integrated picture of people is a clear and concise way to describe his work and identity. As you learn about and are exposed to new theories, think about how they fit into and influence your worldview, if at all. You need to be able to articulate your professional identity with clarity; the statement should link your work to the thought lineages you follow, as well as describe your unique approaches.

Kari Rogenski, when asked to describe her professional identity, sighed and asked if she could do an art piece to represent it instead of words—you may relate to this! Sometimes it is difficult to verbally capture the multifaceted nature of the work creative arts therapists do in the world. Kari described the many different roles she has as a drama therapist: "I am always aware of the different roles and the hats that I wear. When I was younger, this was somewhat anxiety-provoking, because I didn't know what to do with it." She said that now she finds it useful to think about putting on different hats or embodying different roles as a way to switch between her different work functions. She also talked about how beginning a doctoral program and becoming a student again have required another shift in her identity: "What am I doing? Wait, I don't know anything again!" She said it is scary, but at the same time, part of the ongoing process of learning and developing—a process she thinks should continue across your career. Kari conceptualizes this as "embracing being a lifelong student and embracing not-knowing."

In reflecting on the overlap between her work in the seminary and in drama therapy, Tawanna Benbow highlighted the focus on renewal and transformation: "Art is such an organic thing…and so regenerative— when you step into a space and begin to give the room for creativity, things just start to cultivate." We need to find ways to hold on to this feeling of regeneration; Newall wrote about her desire to attain more professional confidence without losing her excitement: "Though I know I am hoping for more comfortable times ahead, I also suspect the raw enthusiasm and bursting passion I feel so often may fade as well" (Junge & Newall, 2015, p. 35). The exercises in this book are geared towards helping you find ways to build your own comfortable and passionate professional identity.

Claiming your knowledge

Being able to describe your specific place in the world furthers both your individual career as well as your disciplines and the creative arts therapies as a whole. In the day-to-day of your job, you may not realize that you are evolving into a specialist. You might also minimize your expertise because of imposter syndrome or phenomena. Feelings of being an imposter in academic or work settings "tends to occur in high achievers and causes them to dismiss, discount or overlook their successes" (Urwin, 2018, p. 1433). Mason (2009) conceptualized imposter syndrome's impact on graduate students as a process that "infiltrates our lives, erodes our self-confidence, thereby creating a disconnection between our selves and our performance abilities as graduate students" (p. 20); the author proposed the use of authentic movement as a means to address feelings of imposter phenomena during training for dance therapists.

Christine Hirabayashi described how she came to understand the unique work she was doing: "I never really thought of myself as an 'experienced therapist' or being in a specialty after being in one place for so long. How much valuable information was there…it wasn't just a job." The process Christine started finding her way through with her clients evolved into an expertise in work with people experiencing chronic pain. The realization that she was having a profound impact on the patients she worked with helped her begin to see herself as an expert.

So how do you go about addressing feelings of being an imposter?

After conducting an exploratory study of imposter phenomena (IP) in social workers, Urwin (2018) recommended addressing misconceptions about experience and expertise head-on:

> We often view successful people as "superhuman", achieving success without effort due to their skills and abilities. Deconstructing these myths and recognizing that success is difficult to achieve and struggling is not a sign of failure may lessen the impact of IP. (p. 1443)

Acknowledging the process you are engaged in to build your therapeutic and artistic expertise is an important part of building your professional identity.

 What knowledge do you have that is or is building towards expertise?

What words or phrases would you use to describe your expertise?

What would it take to use these words or phrases aloud to someone in the next few weeks?

Portability of professional self

Moving away from the state, region, or country where you study can present difficulties when it comes to licensure and job outreach. Hadas Weissberg described her dilemma when she moved to California from the Boston area; her situation is one many creative arts therapists face when moving:

> Since I'm here in the Bay Area, I haven't worked as a dance therapist. The process to become a marriage and family therapist or Licensed Professional Clinical Counselor it is so difficult. In the beginning, I was working on my Ph.D, so I didn't find anything. But then recently I started to send all this stuff to the Board of Behavioral Sciences and found out that I need to complete so many classes so I didn't start doing it. Now I'm thinking about what to do next because it is so many classes and all the classes are expensive. It feels so weird, because in Boston I could apply for the Licensed Mental Health Counselor [accreditation], but here

is so much different. I still didn't figure out what I'm going to do; I'm working now at the Jewish Community Center in Palo Alto as a program manager there.

She said she is very happy in her role at the Jewish Community Center, but feels increasingly strong feelings about missing doing the work of a dance therapist. She recently completed her Ph.D and is in the process of deciding what to do next. The uncertainty is unfortunately part of the process for many, especially after moving from one area to another.

The clearer you can be about where you want to practice and the type of work you want to do should help you make decisions and prepare for as many possible paths as you can.

Having an idea about where you want to live and the type of work you want to do will enable you to make early choices to support your professional goals. Changing your mind or needing to move unexpectedly are not insurmountable, but require that you acknowledge the realities. Dual licensure has created opportunities for creative arts therapists, but it can be a double-edged sword; it may dilute or confuse your professional identity. Junge and Newall (2015) wrote about this possible confusion in art therapy, where the student or new professional may not get as in-depth instruction as is needed in the service of meeting requirements for multiple licensing bodies. On the other hand, pursuing multiple qualifications can enable you to pursue a range of job opportunities.

Denise Wolf described how her need for and pursuit of licenses and credentialing shifted along with her career focus: "Earlier on, when I thought I was going to go into school-based services, I was more interested in pursuing my special education certification and all those educational certificates." When she began teaching, her mentors suggested she should get her board certification and clinical supervision credential and also state licensure as a Licensed Professional Counselor. She did warn about losing sight of your identity as a creative arts therapist when you are doing other kinds of work: "Hold your identity as an art therapist. I think a lot of art therapists end up kind of doing verbal therapy and the art is an aside." She said that some of the reasons she hears are that the client does not want to make art or that the therapist does not do art with certain clients. She recommended maintaining a strong connection, at least internally or in the way you talk about your work, to the art media and practices: "That is our first identity and our strongest tool."

Kari Rogenski spoke about the process she went through, having gone back and forth between California and Canada for school and during her process of getting licensure in marriage and family therapy (MFT):

My licensing journey was really hard. It was probably the most taxing thing I've had to do in my life, and I've had to do some pretty taxing things in my life! For whatever reason, my MFT license journey hit every loophole and pothole possible.

When she first graduated, her background and experience in California did not qualify her for licensure in Canada, so she took the jobs she could get while she figured out what she really wanted to do. She started taking some classes in order to meet the licensure requirements in Canada while working two jobs, seven days a week, "just to try to find my footing, get grounded." Later she moved back to California where she was able to be licensed as a marriage and family therapist—but it was a long journey. She identified an upside to this struggle to get licensed: "What it taught me is to appreciate the importance of keeping records." She described herself as very type-A about her continuing education records and license because she does not want them to lapse. She keeps meticulous records, both in hard copy and digital files, and she also recommends keeping records in multiple places, particularly when your licensing is in-process.

Your peers and your professional network are very important as you work towards credentials, certifications, and licenses. Not only are they important in that they may be signing off on your hours, providing references, or verifying your education; they also provide support in other ways. I have heard from students that they find it very helpful to have a "buddy" who is walking along the journey with them—someone in their same supervision group or who graduated at the same time.

They share tips, encourage each other, and celebrate each milestone. Consider who you might pair up with to study for a board certification exam or fill out paperwork.

Collaboration with other creative arts therapists

Collaborations bring opportunities for inspiration and give you a deeper appreciation for all the modalities. They create opportunity to expand your awareness of your clients beyond the input you usually get.

When you work together with others as a creative arts therapist, you can enrich your clients' experiences and your own work.

Collaboration with a drama therapist and dance movement therapist while working at a children's hospital gave me more awareness and attunement to the ways my clients held their bodies and moved during individual art therapy sessions because I had seen them in movement-based sessions. My interactions became much more embodied than they had been previously. Hadas Weissberg spoke of a similar development through collaboration with an art therapist: "It was empowering for me—it helped me to create my tools in a better and deeper way." Kari Rogenski sees collaboration between creative arts therapists as a way forward for the field as a whole: "I've been very disheartened in my career regarding the animosity between the creative arts therapies disciplines. I think it is very unsavory and it is what is holding us back." She spoke about the need for people in all the creative arts therapies to collaborate on things like licensure and job security and title protection.

Two of the contributors to this book, Christine Hirabayashi, an art therapist, and Collen Lorenz, a dance therapist, collaborated on a multi-stage process involving visual art, music, dance, and audience participation. Christine described the collaboration as "such an interesting experience, and an unexpected one." She met Coleen at a salon talk during her doctoral education and initiated a conversation about collaborating:

I was thinking about how art tells a story, but dance is a different way to tell a story and it is in their bodies and working with people with chronic pain, to have them be able to express their pain through their own interpretation.

Instantly, they knew they had an idea they wanted to explore together— bringing Christine's artists with chronic pain together with Colleen's dancers. They invited an artist Christine worked with to bring his art in to show the dancers. The dancers chose the art that they wanted to create dance from. The visual artist in turn, watched the individual dancers on stage and created new visual art in response. One of the dancers was injured during the process, so she created the musical score for the performance. Audience members were also involved and able to respond to the performance and exhibition. Christine Hirabayashi spoke about what she learned from the collaboration:

It opened me up to a different form of art, using the body. Working with people who had chronic pain, I had even more of an appreciation for the dance part of things, and how combined with the visual, how powerful it could be. Not only for the performer and the artist but for the audience that was watching. It was so multilayered.

The two have engaged in subsequent multidisciplinary collaborations, inviting audience members in to create visual art in response to previews of performances, which are then exhibited during the performance run.

When asked what lessons creative arts therapists should take from their project, Christine Hirabayashi encouraged people to reach out to others, participate in other disciplines' projects, see their performances or exhibitions, and make connections. She stated:

Think out of the box and see how creativity works on many different levels. When you are able to collaborate, it creates a stronger voice for the piece. And it reaches a much more diverse group. It feels like you're not so alone. It's the solidarity of being able to come together and just create something. There's no words to explain it, really! When you do think out of the box, it just becomes all that much more meaningful. We all take in the world in different ways. It seems more purposeful when you work in collaboration with others versus trying to do something on your own. There's so much more possibility that opens up and it feels much more purposeful.

She described this collaborative, multidisciplinary work as a way to "explain the unexplainable."

If you are wondering where and how to start these collaborations, consider how you might use internet networking and social media (Miller, 2017) as a means to connect with like-minded creative arts therapists. Donna Newman-Bluestein expressed how useful she has found this strategy: "I'm very active in social media in connecting with the creative arts therapies field. There's so much richness." One example of this richness is an online art exchange group described by art therapists (Chilton et al., 2009); the project was a place for them to meet as artists and to cultivate "connectedness and optimism" (p. 71). Jess Minckley created art about the benefits of collaborating with others (Figure 8.1). She emphasized the importance of sharing different experiences and perspectives:

"Stronger Together" is about diversity and inclusion leading to greater unity. We strengthen as we share different perspectives with one another. This is a matter of respect, and it also fuels our efforts in social justice and advocating for change and reform discipline-wide. We cannot do the important work we do in our larger society without being fed as people. Community feeds our souls as individuals. Discourse helps us grow as a group. Inclusion of divergent perspectives is imperative—our field must be unified as we walk into the future together.

 How can you feed your soul as Jess Minckley suggested? Who might you collaborate with, now or in the future? Be sure you take care of and tend to those possible collaborative relationships.

Figure 8.1 "Stronger Together"—digital drawing by Jess Minckley

Everyone you meet along your path is someone you might collaborate with in the future. Kari Rogenski nurtures these potential collaborative connections by sending handwritten thank-yous to people she's connected with: "The notes say things like 'thank you for what you taught me today' or 'what you shared with me today' or 'for making me feel comfortable at this meeting we attended.'" She emphasized the need to preserve the importance of the personal touch as you navigate connecting with peers and mentors, keeping in mind that you should express gratitude given these people's busy schedules: "They're doing this out of the goodness of their heart; they're not doing it because they have a bunch of extra time and resources. They're doing it because they want you to be successful." Building collaborative relationships with other creative arts therapists has many benefits, one of which is exposure to the kindness and collegiality among your peers.

Collaboration with allied professionals

Collaboration with other artists and creative professionals can yield exciting and nourishing results, both for the clients and professionals. Denise Wolf cautioned that creative arts therapists should not be "dismissive or reactionary" to allied professionals of other backgrounds doing work with groups of people: "We don't own the use of art, and we use words as well." She suggested your responsibility as a good collaborator is to help other allied professionals use the arts in ethical ways. You may also collaborate with other health- and mental health-care workers, as closely allied peers in your work.

I have written previously about the many benefits to collaboration with fine arts and design students (Partridge, 2019c). Over the last decade, I have had the opportunity for long-term collaboration with Sadie Harmon. We met when Sadie started volunteering in the older adult community where I worked, then she became a coworker when we had a job opening. And now several years later, we are coworkers again in the business development and strategy department of our nonprofit. Working with my community arts colleague has been one of my richest collaborations. We share a common language of the arts and a passion for working in community with older adults. Our recent collaborations include a workshop at an art therapy conference, an art-based exploration with a person living with dementia, and a grant-funded research project. While walking back to our hotel after a meal during a conference, one of our colleagues acknowledged our similar orientation to the world around us: "It is so interesting walking around with you two; you notice everything!" She observed that we were commenting on funny signs and street art we passed on our walk. Having someone else in your workplace who speaks a shared language of the arts is especially helpful when you are in a non-traditional role or setting.

Sometimes your collaborations will necessitate thinking about how your role is perceived by others. Fatmah Al-Qadfan spoke about the joy and creative fulfilment she gains from collaboration in non-therapy theater and drama settings, but also the need for engaging in code switching as a drama therapist walking into those spaces:

> Suddenly, I'm walking into a rehearsal space or meeting actors, and being introduced as the therapist, and that's kind of alienating. Because suddenly, I'm not one of them. But I am! That's where I started and that's where I identify, maybe even more than to the therapist/psychotherapist community.

She recently experienced this difference in perception while collaborating on a large theater production; she was asked to come in to train the child actor in the show. She said she was often misidentified as a speech therapist or occupational therapist, which she would correct and then explain her role; she told people she was there to "tap into the child's creativity" during rehearsal, "filling in the gaps for her." She loved the collaboration, but acknowledged that other people were confused by her presence; the experience highlighted another area to educate about the work and scope of drama therapy.

You will benefit from your professional collaborations, but may have to let go of some of the control you would have working alone. Kari Rogenski shared about how she navigated developing a truly collaborative practice:

> My training program focused on becoming my own private practitioner. It wasn't about collaboration: there was nothing about business, nothing about paying your taxes or how to employ someone. I always felt steered to wanting to own my ideas. I really had to get over that.

She spoke about coming to the realization that some of the ideas she brought to her work were her own ideas and some were the founder's ideas, and in all cases, their work needed to be in support of the larger organization. When she shifted to thinking about the project and the mission of their work, things improved: "This idea of needing to own the most original idea just dissolved for me. We may have these brilliant ideas, but in order for them to grow, we have to share." Her advice may assist you in thinking about how sharing ideas and collaborating with others can help you expand your work to a larger audience or have greater impact on communities.

Sharing Ideas and Knowledge

What does originality and ownership mean to you in the context of your work?

· ·

· ·

· ·

What do you learn through collaboration and sharing?

· ·

· ·

· ·

How much of your work feels proprietary versus how much feels open-source or part of the collective knowledge?

· ·

· ·

· ·

How does collaboration and sharing support your clients, communities, or research work?

· ·

· ·

· ·

Andra Duncan shared the ways collaboration with caregiving and nursing staff in a skilled nursing setting was a turning point for her—both in her relationship with coworkers and in her own professional identity. She described how her efforts to communicate about what she does as a music therapist gave her coworkers a baseline of information that guided them to seek her out when an older adult in the skilled-nursing environment needed comfort or soothing. They began to treat her as "part of the fabric of the community." She said that staff would alert her when they noticed someone in need of some extra attention or psychosocial support. Andra fostered this relationship further by recognizing and encouraging the talents of her coworkers:

> One thing that was really interesting to me and that I loved, when you're working with non-creative arts therapists, when you're working with assistants or paraprofessionals or nursing staff, is being able to notice and recognize, support, and encourage their talents. So noticing they were singing down the hallway while they walked and encouraging that talent. I would encourage singing with the resident or playing an instrument, and I would have team-building where I would often encourage them to play an instrument. A lot of the staff members I've worked with have been talented that way in their own lives, where they enjoy singing in choirs, or enjoy playing instruments... maybe they play guitar. They may not want to show me that because they're intimidated in a certain way. It was really great when I was able to notice these things because then I could encourage them... I'm only there eight or ten hours a day, they're there overnight. Being able to share what I do without feeling like someone else is taking that away. Because they're not minimizing what I do as a music therapist: they're augmenting what I'm already doing and they're learning some techniques.

Andra Duncan's collaborative, non-hierarchical approach enabled an improved working relationship with the nursing and care staff and a greater ability to support their older adult clients. Another music therapist used telehealth technology and a collaborative treatment approach with a psychologist to provide music therapy to a veteran with PTSD

(Lightstone, Bailey, & Voros, 2015). New technologies can facilitate collaborations that might not otherwise be possible.

 Talented Coworkers _____

What talents have you noticed in your peers and coworkers that you could nurture and support?

How could you support them in expressing those talents?

How could you support them in developing new talents?

Collaboration outside the field

If you are open, you can find ways to collaborate with people from all different backgrounds and settings—doing the bridge-building work Carolan (2001) described: "We cannot be satisfied with demanding that they learn our language. We must be bridge builders, and research is a critical building block" (p. 191). Your ability to collaborate with people in vastly different fields is only limited by your imagination and networks. A series of events led to a very fruitful collaboration with people in a seemingly unrelated field to my own. Part of my role includes serving as a liaison between older adults and people developing new technology; we have hosted focus groups and pilot explorations of many different technology types—from smartphone apps to robots. This area of my work included informal use of a social robot in several of our communities. Some early attention from local media (Halstead, 2018) caught the attention of the people developing the robot. They reached out to learn more, and our conversations about what I was observing prompted us to initiate a formal research study (Ostrowski et al., 2019). The first study involved hosting four robots in one of our communities for several weeks, running discussion groups, and doing art-based responses to the robot.

In the process of designing the study, doing data analysis, and writing our results, the roboticists, design researchers, and I developed a very collaborative and inspiring partnership. Upon completion of our initial study, we began a second inquiry. We are also discussing future partnerships to incorporate art therapy and arts-based inquiry into human–robot interaction and human–computer interaction research. Throughout the process, I strengthened my voice as an art therapy researcher—growing into new abilities to make the case for inclusion of arts-based methods and to speak to people in unrelated fields about the work of the arts therapies.

I found our collaborations extremely valuable. Conversations with these collaborators have exposed me to ideas and literature I may never have encountered. Our data analysis processes have strengthened my commitment to participatory research processes and have revealed to me new means to achieve interrater reliability and consensus. Writing up the art-based portion of our study enabled me to think about new audiences for art therapy research. In doing this work, we discovered we were not the first technology design and art therapy partnership (Lazar et al., 2016).

 ## Interdisciplinary Collaboration

Think of a field or discipline that seems completely unrelated to your own.

Create a Venn diagram using words, line, shape, and colors to represent your field in one circle and the other, unrelated field in the other circle. Consider the following questions as you fill in the space where the circles overlap:

- Where do your circles overlap?

- What does that overlap consist of?

- How might your work inform theirs and vice versa?

- How could you collaborate?

Hint: Collage can be really helpful in doing this exercise.

Collaborating with clients

You might also collaborate with clients at different points in your career, where it is ethically and therapeutically appropriate to do so. At the most basic level, your interactions with clients are a collaboration—you are engaged in a therapeutic relationship that is a collaboration, as studied in music therapy sessions (Rolvsjord, 2016), where the researcher focused on the client's contributions. The author identified promising trends towards more acknowledgement of the interaction or collaborative nature of therapy, but recommended placing greater emphasis on client collaboration in session. Talwar (2019b) also wrote about the collaboration between therapists and clients: "Collaborations are messy encounters and regularly reveal lessons in power" (p. 187). Some processes involve increased collaboration and trust between therapist and client. Ceramics is one example, particularly when you as the therapist are operating the kiln. The process of bisque and glaze firing can be seen as a collaboration between client and therapist—with a positive outcome when the firing goes well, and a difficult-to-navigate but potentially therapeutically useful outcome when the firing does not go to plan.

You will also collaborate with clients in developing, writing, and working towards treatment goals. You may help your clients identify things they have said in the past that are good goals to work for, framed within the scope of work you can do together. Where possible, use the clients' own words to describe their goals: hearing direct quotes in their care-planning meetings or as you talk about progress with them can really build trust and rapport. Denise Wolf encourages her students to work collaboratively with their clients in each session:

> You might go into session with an idea, but you're going to meet your client where they are, you're going to talk with them, and you're going to have access to everything you know about art media and processes, about neurobiology and the expressive therapies continuum.

She said this approach takes some time to feel comfortable—sometimes students and new professionals want to feel "armored" with a planned-out directive.

Christine Hirabayashi has facilitated an open studio for clients who graduate from a structured treatment program for chronic pain. The open studio members produce a yearly exhibit. They write artist statements to be displayed with their work; these statements often describe how participating in art therapy and the aftercare studio supports their recovery. She described the impact of this work: "I think beyond just the collaboration with the group members, what it did was that the open studio provided a place to be creative, but beyond that, being there for the opening gave them something to be proud of." She spoke about the artists having an opportunity to see themselves as artists, not patients with chronic pain. Their artists' statements tell the story of the power of art therapy—what it meant in their restoration process or in coming to terms with their circumstances: "You get to understand the beauty of what is underlying art therapy—the power of it." In describing the exhibit, she noted therapists do not ask clients directly about what art therapy means to them; they look for therapeutic progress, and may engage in retrospective sessions or conversations with clients (Nash, 2017), but rarely reflect on the bigger picture of the work or provide opportunities to express to the public. The collaborative art show invites clients to express themselves and share their stories. In a study of experiences of art making, researchers adopted participatory practices to more directly collaborate with people with mental illnesses in understanding their experiences (Van Lith, Fenner, & Schofield, 2011). When you collaborate with clients or former clients, you can tell larger stories about the impact of the work you do.

Your whole self

A question that comes up in hiring or contracting contexts is what skills creative arts therapists will bring to the table. When applying and interviewing for a job with my current organization, interviewers repeatedly asked, "Okay, so you'll do some art, but what *else* can you do?" In the moment, I listed off a whole range of interests as I fumed inside—insulted they did not yet understand the capabilities and the scope of work I could do. I felt both excited to bring my whole self to work and upset at their initial dismissal of art therapy as not enough for a full-time position.

Fatmah Al-Qadfan described facing the same question as she sought to establish herself as a drama therapist in Kuwait. Educating employers about your field will help with some of the incorrect assumptions, but demonstrating through your actions has more impact. While maintaining your professional integrity is essential, you should not overlook the balance and professional satisfaction you can gain by incorporating other interests into your work. Where possible, incorporating other skills and interests into your portfolio makes you a valuable asset.

✎ Skills and Interests Beyond Clinical Practice _____

Write down a list of all your interests and skills—write down as many as you can think of, big and small. Some of them may seem obscure and possibly unrelated to your work, but write them down anyway.

. . . .

. . . .

. . . .

. . . .

. . . .

Once you have your list, mark the skills you already use in your activities with an asterisk.

Circle the skills and interests that you do not currently use at work, but upon reflection might easily integrate into what you do. Make some notes to yourself about how you might facilitate a group or approach work with a certain client using a specific skill.

Underline the skills and interests that seem totally unrelated to your work. Are there other ways you can think about and express those skills? For example, baking may not be possible or appropriate in your current workplace, but perhaps it is part of your self-care or is a way to connect with and support coworkers.

Keep this list of interests and skills in mind when you meet new clients—it may be the bridge to developing rapport and a therapeutic relationship with them!

One of the difficulties you may face as a creative arts therapist is the preconceived ideas your clients bring to therapy. They may have lifelong beliefs that they are not creative, cannot carry a tune, have two left feet, and other negative self-statements. A strategy for establishing rapport with clients is to introduce adjacent shared interests. Talking with a client who never came to the art studio about our mutual love for birds created an opportunity to invite him into creative contexts. He never made any art with me, but he did attend several art shows focused on birds and nature—invitations I was able to make because we had been discussing birds for months. On the ride back to the community after one trip, he shared with the other older adults that he had never been to an art exhibit that he understood and felt connected to before. When I was helping him step down from the van at the end of our journey home, he asked me to please be sure to invite him again.

Finding ways to bring more of myself into my work with older adults has helped me make deep connections with them. Context may preclude any personal story sharing, but does not eliminate the possibility for discussing other areas of interest beyond the immediate therapeutic work and the art discipline you utilize. These diversified discussions can model for your clients that you are not just one thing, and by extension, neither are they.

Working within a forensic hospital requires strict personal boundaries and can seem like the least likely place to bring your whole self. However, with good professional boundaries and clarity about your intention, you are able to talk about things beyond the therapy without disclosing any personal information.

In the case of one very difficult individual on my caseload at a state hospital, discussing things outside therapy and rehabilitation was a means to invite him into contemplation of the therapeutic process. Learning about his interest in creating a fashion line based on a favorite slang statement, I began talking with him about graphic design and silkscreening, gradually building a rapport as evidenced by his ceasing to call me one of his many creative curse-word-filled names and instead calling me by my first name when addressing me in the hallway. We talked several times on the unit about his ideas, and I suggested he check out the unit's set of colored pencils to sketch some of his ideas. After a few weeks of this work, I described the materials available to him in the art studio: "You're here, and we have supplies. You should use them while they're available to you—they're expensive on the outside."

I also enlisted the rest of the unit's interdisciplinary team in encouraging his entrepreneurship. I showed him examples of different ways he could silkscreen his design ideas and described, as best I could, the new technology he could access once on the outside. After a while longer in contemplation, he agreed to register for the open studio in his next treatment team meeting. Our whole interdisciplinary team was shocked when he followed through on the request—most of us had doubted he would show up. He came to the studio once or twice, but ultimately decided his commitment to eschewing treatment was stronger than his desire for the use of good materials. It was not lost effort, however, because he continued to work on his designs and we continued to have a positive rapport. Sharing my knowledge and history in graphic design enabled a better therapeutic relationship with this individual.

Shifting identities

Your entire professional identity may involve different titles, names, labels, and roles. These aspects of identity shift over time and according to context. Tawanna Benbow described her professional identity as a wheel with many spokes, an image that serves as a useful metaphor to explore.

Wheel Directive

Prior to doing this directive, you might benefit from doing some brainstorming or freewriting to generate ideas.

Write or collage words, phrases, or other descriptors related to your professional identity on the spokes of the wheel.

If there is a word, title, phrase, or image that feels most central to your professional identity, put that in the center of the wheel.

Fill the rim of the wheel with words, phrases, colors, or images related to what moves you forward—what stimulates progress.

You might also decide to add color or imagery to the spaces between the wheel spokes.

Add the environment to this page—where is this wheel rolling through?

Consider any barriers to forward motion—what obstacles might be in the path of this wheel? Are there ways over or around those obstacles?

Where has the wheel been, and where is it headed?

The different spokes of your professional identity will shift and change over time. Returning to this metaphor across your career will help you identify areas of growth and opportunities for continued professional development. You might consider using this exercise each year, either at the turn of the New Year or prior to performance evaluations in your workplace, as a way to check in and set intentions about where you want to go in the next year. You might also use it to guide you in times of transition—changing jobs or taking on new responsibilities in your existing role.

Expanding your practice beyond a specialty can also be a means to grow, as described by Christine Hirabayashi. She talked about the benefit she saw when she began working with clients beyond the chronic pain clinic where she spent most of her early career:

> It makes me realize what I'm really interested in. I love working with all the clients I do. It keeps me learning new things. It helps me learn not just more about art and art therapy. It opens my eyes to life. It keeps me grounded in the whole experience of human beings.

As Hadas Weissberg discussed, there may be times when your professional identity is not dictated by your professional role. There may be times in your career where you are not working or your role is not related to the practice of creative arts therapies. Periods of time where you are doing family work, coping with health issues, in-between roles, or in school or training for your next opportunity do not erase your professional identity. Andra Duncan spoke about her important realization that she was "always a music therapist" no matter her present employment status. The recent global pandemic has created a need to reinvent work with clients, and in some cases has limited the ability to do the work creative arts therapists are trained to do. These changes and limitations do not alter who you are at the core of your professional identity.

Continuing education

Attending and participating in continuing education is essential, and not just to maintain licenses and certifications. You should use continuing education as a means to stay current on best practices, to connect with others, and to explore emerging lines of research. Attending conferences or other trainings is especially impactful if you are the only creative arts therapist in your setting: getting to spend time with colleagues mitigates some of the professional loneliness you may feel. Loneliness in the workplace can arise when there is a gap between what you want from your relationships there and what you currently experience; it is "the negative discrepancy between actual and desired relationships at work, and the inability to rectify this imbalance" (Wright, Burt, & Strongman,

2006, p. 60). Attending conferences cannot address the imbalance in the day-to-day, but can help you feel a part of a larger whole. Where possible, take the opportunity to connect with others who work with the same population you do or in similar settings—there are often peer groups or specific networking opportunities for this purpose.

Accessing resources for continuing education can be difficult when you move away from locations with training programs. Additionally, though you can get many continuing education credits at once at a large national or international conference, this option is prohibitively expensive for many, especially those who are new to the field or who do not have access to training support via their employer. Fatmah Al-Qadfan talked about budgeting to ensure her ability to attend conferences along with other lower-cost means to engage in professional development:

> I stay up to date by attending the annual drama therapy conference, reading the *Drama Therapy Review*, and staying in touch with my peers. I also take classes online on best practices and treatment modalities in approaching eating disorders and complex trauma. I feel like conferences are vital to my professional survival! I set a budget aside each year and use some of my annual leave days to make sure that I attend and connect with my peers.

Her voice was full of joy as she described what attending the annual conference means to her.

 Think back to what you learned in Chapter 2 about how you learn and grow. Does a week of intensive sessions at a national conference meet your needs? Or would you prefer to do shorter courses spaced out across the year?

Kari Rogenski shared a tactic she uses to make sure she gets the most benefit out of her continuing education: she chooses sessions and settings for continuing education that "cross-pollinate" by satisfying the requirements for her marriage and family therapy license as well as drama therapy.

What else can you gain from conferences? After attending her first national conference in our field, a student in my research course expressed how inspired she felt and how that inspiration translated into motivation for completing her thesis research; she wanted to finish so she could present it and be part of the dialogue.

To make the most of your conference experience, seek out information beforehand and resources while attending, and follow up on connections afterwards.

If you are considering attending a conference you have not attended before, see if you can make contact with people who have been in previous years. Find out which aspects of the conference are not to be missed and which parts you can skip if you are tired or need some time for yourself. Once you are there, keep track of what you gain from the experience; these insights can help you advocate for more training opportunities in the future. Remember to pace yourself—you do not have to attend every session or every networking opportunity and you will exhaust yourself trying!

When asked about his own continuing education since his return to Saudi Arabia, Fahad al Fahed used himself as an example of the larger need in his country—a chicken/egg argument about whether there is a need to first develop a training program or first develop resources and rules to govern art therapy: "That's part of the problem. I'm trying to be part of the mental health mission here." He said that some people see it as part of "just art" while others see it as part of psychology or counseling. He is working to be part of the clarification efforts and the solution, but it will not change overnight. The increasing prevalence of online continuing education and learning and virtual conferences[1] can help fill in the gaps in the meantime.

---

1   See, for example, www.dicats.org/about

137

Funding continuing education

Discussing the need for financial support for continuing education and professional development is important—making clear to your supervisor or to leadership that part of hiring a creative arts therapist requires providing opportunities for continuing education. Early in my work for a nonprofit organization, I was not able to negotiate having my conference fees covered, but I was able to make requests for the release time from work—no small feat for an hourly employee. Later, as I learned who to talk to, I was able to get reimbursement for conference fees. In my current position with this same company, all my travel and fees are budgeted for and covered, including trips to international conferences.

My approach to advocating for my professional development was twofold. First, I provided information and education about my credential and board certification and the requirements for recertification. I connected my professional requirement to the clinical work; serving our clients requires professional maintenance. Second, I made the case for the impact of professional presentations. You have to put your business hat on for this conversation—roles you may feel more or less comfortable with. Presenting creates natural marketing opportunities for your organization or employer, both on the side of seeking new clients as well as recruiting for open or future positions. Presenting about your work is also a way to advocate for the client population you serve or to educate about issues your clients experience. In my case, my organization's interest in being seen as a thought-leading organization in fighting ageism is an excellent focus for my conference attendance.

Think about what organizational goals you could support via conference attendance and presentations. You might have this conversation with your supervisor in your department or with a different department that has outreach or advocacy goals. For example, you may be able to advocate for attending a conference if you offer to help staff a table for your organization or to bring fliers about open positions.

Additional training and education

The decision to seek additional training can arise from many different stimuli. Christine Hirabayashi described the process of deciding to pursue a Ph.D in art therapy:

> Ten years in the field, I had heard about the Ph.D program... I was kind of bored with the job, there were some internal challenges. I'm either going to quit my job because I need something different... I'm just going to apply and see what happens. And then realizing more about the program and starting to understand the impact it could really make in other people's lives and the need for it... Then I knew, this is where I'm supposed to be.

Her realization was similar to those expressed by many contributors to this book—the "ah-ha" moment or sense of sureness about the next step.

Pursuing further education might require you to pause your clinical work. Hadas Weissberg said that her doctoral work enabled her to feel close to the field, though she was not employed as a dance movement therapist at the time. She said it remains part of her identity, even though she felt a little behind as a clinician because she put that part of her career on pause. Taking a pause may be the best ethical step—both for yourself and for your clients. Pursuing higher education while doing clinical work can put a great deal of pressure on you and can impact your ability to be present for your clients. However, sometimes your financial situation or the job market may require you to find ways to make it work.

I did not work during my master's program, which allowed me to focus on the coursework, personal development, and clinical training, but I did work full-time throughout my Ph.D. At times, it was so exhausting I wondered if I could make it; I was very aware of how precarious my situation was. One bad flu during the final months of my dissertation work put me into a catastrophic situation with paid time off—I had none left to use and was too sick to go to work, especially since I worked with medically vulnerable older adults. My immune system seemed to sense the light at the end of the long tunnel and was giving up early, or more likely was responding to several years of escalating stress. However, I was able to work it out with our HR department. They reduced my pay and approved the time out sick even though I had no more paid time off. I was very lucky to be in a position where I could work with my supervisors on a solution and could financially survive a cut in my pay for that pay period. When you are planning how you will structure your life while you pursue more education, do not forget to account for caring for your physical body. Think about what safety nets you can construct prior to engaging in additional training or study.

Personal Safety Nets

What practices, rituals, and behaviors are essential to your physical and psychosocial wellbeing? What safety nets can you put in place to ensure these needs are met and you will have support?

....
....
....
....
....

Who could you ask for support and encouragement?

....
....
....
....
....

Supervision

Hadas Weissberg described how her early experiences with a great supervisor, as well as group supervision with many dance movement therapists (DMTs) with differing levels of experience, enabled her to better understand the work she was doing:

> What really was helpful working as a dance movement therapist was that there were many DMTs meeting every month. It was very helpful, because there were so many experienced dance movement therapists while I was just at the beginning. It was so helpful because we danced together and then talked a little bit. It's such an open field—it's not like "this thing that you need to do and it will make everything all good"—it's not like that so it can be confusing.

Having many peers to process workplace experiences with is so helpful, particularly because of the uncertainty about what our work entails, as Hadas Weissberg identified. Supervision is an important place for navigating conflicts between highly regimented and structured settings and your creative arts therapy work. We had weekly group supervision in a state hospital setting where I worked, and having the time and space to make art together while we processed the often difficult setting where we worked was so essential. For other work settings or populations, having individual or group supervision comprising people from other contexts can help provide you with a different perspective.

Denise Wolf spoke about the importance of ongoing peer supervision, both formal and informal. She hosts a monthly supervision that is heavily art-based and encourages accountability for attendees making their own art. Participants in the supervision identify a theme, create artist trading cards,[2] and then swap cards with each other. This monthly supervision group also ensures she will have some form of art practice in each month: "If nothing else, if art making doesn't show up in my month, I know it will show up in supervision." Similar to the use of ritual discussed in Chapter 1, having rituals and patterns involving professional development can help you make it a priority.

---

2   See www.strathmoreartist.com/cards-atc.html

CHAPTER 9

Creative and Artistic Identity

Maintaining a connection to your creative, expressive self is essential in the creative arts therapies field. Your licenses and board certifications mandate certain levels of continuing education; you need to treat the maintenance of this creative, expressive self with just as much importance. How this importance manifests will differ for each individual and will change as your career changes. This chapter includes the ethical and self-care reasons for maintaining one's sense of artistic identity in the creative arts therapies. It covers continuing education in the arts, developing a personal creative practice as a form of self-care, and the use of creative practice in research. Topics such as performance or exhibitions, networking, and exploration/inspiration are also included.

Creativity as self-care

Exercising your creative self can bring balance into your life. One of the things I love about work with older adults is their long view on what matters in life and their emphasis on balance. One woman, a retired educator, put it well: "People can be too serious—no life in their life!" Healthy patterns help to keep the life in our lives, and focusing on your creative identity is a way to do that.

Think about what brought you to the creative arts in the first place. What did you get from the song, the movement, the stage, or the brushstroke?

Donna Newman-Bluestone identified what called her to dance therapy:

> So in some ways when I found the field of dance therapy, I was really drawn to the physicality. It was something that I desperately needed—to be grounded in my own physical being. So dance was the art form I was most drawn to because I think I needed it the most.

Gillam (2018) wrote about the close connection between wellbeing and creativity and the "importance of creativity to mental health and wellbeing, the survival of the reflective, creative practitioner, and the problem of occupational stress and satisfying professional practice" (p. 5). Having experienced the powerful role art can play in personal reflection, growth, and community building, which led me to art therapy, it is important to me that I maintain opportunities for myself to access those aspects of art.

The Support of Creativity

Here are some questions to think about or do some writing about as you consider the role that creativity and the arts play in your life.

How does creativity support your professional identity?

How does creativity support your personal identity?

How does creativity support your physical health?

How does creativity support your mental health?

How does creativity support you in your community?

Your creative practices may be closely tied to your work and thereby to the associated stress or difficulty. They are also deeply important to who you are in the world, making it hard to step away from work. As Hadas Weissberg said, "I think the creative is in me and I bring it to everything that I do." You need mental breaks, where you take time away from your work and your workplace roles. Fosslien and Duffy (2019) wrote about the difficulty of taking a real break from our work identities: "You're emotionally attached to that self because you've spent a lot of time together!" (p. 27). They go on to recommend being careful about bringing workplace approaches to the things you enjoy.

In a study of the off-work activities of health-care workers, de Jonge, Shimazu, and Dollard (2018) found workers were unable to adequately emotionally and cognitively detach from work if they engaged in work-related activities outside of working hours. As a creative arts therapist, you need to be careful that your leisure-based arts engagement is not work-related. Fuzzy boundaries between work studio and home studio may mean making grief-work about a patient who died, bringing client art to home studio, replaying music from emotionally charged sessions, or bringing topics appropriate for peer supervision into your creative practice. You can address this by being intentional about incorporating time for arts-based processing at work. Doing the arts-based processing related to clients at work or supervision means more space for doing creative self-exploration that is just for you outside of work hours.

Donna Newman-Bluestein also suggested diversifying the approaches you take to creative practice: "I perform in a small, intergenerational dance company. I go to performances, museums, and really fill myself with inspiration. I just keep feeding myself so that I am nurtured and nourished so that I have something to give." She went on to talk about how these forms of creative nurturance happened both in groups and independently:

I do different things at different times. I take dance classes. Sometimes I will have a period of doing visual art. I read memoirs of people who inspire me. I'm also part of a creativity group, and we meet monthly and share with each other.

When you are setting patterns for yourself, consider how you might engage in both group and individual creative practices, and the different benefits you would gain from each.

Kari Rogenski tries to make it as simple as possible to squeeze creative practices into her daily life:

> I do have an art space in my office. I had this grand idea of starting my creativity studies Ph.D program and doing a collage every day. Most days, I have one piece of paper out, and most days I've got a marker and I'm doing a squiggle as I'm brushing my teeth and running out the door. But I get the squiggle on the page and art is born of that.

She spoke about how creativity contributes to her self-care and the need to find ways to work it into each day, in whatever form that might take: "Sometimes self-care is getting the water in the water bottle and then—important step—the water bottle into my bag before I go. I think being humble around not having pressure about what the creativity needs to be." Kari also spoke about exploring different forms of creative practice as a way to push herself. At the time of the interview for this book, she had started taking singing lessons:

> It makes me so nervous! I will dance backwards on stage for you, but singing lessons is not my strength. But as a creative arts therapist, it is so important to do things outside my box—because every day I ask a client to do that.

She explained that while you might have a clinical awareness that your clients have fears and anxieties about engaging in the work of expressive therapy, you can forget about what it actually feels like unless you are regularly engaged in your own lived experience: "It is great in that moment to be reminded of the rawness. And to sing and sound beautiful or horrible. It doesn't matter, because you're there to learn." Consider exploring a creative practice that can stimulate some of that fear or anxiety or newness. What does it feel like to be a beginner again?

 Think about a creative practice that is outside your current skillset or therapeutic work; it might be an interest you had in childhood or in your early career or something you have never done before.

Set aside some time to explore as a beginner again. As you do, reflect on the experiences, both positive and negative, of learning or exploring someone outside of your comfort zone.

With regard to her creative and artistic self, Denise Wolf utilizes several tactics to maintain her identity as an artist. She brings a small sketchbook with her most places she goes, and loves to "visit art museums, plop myself down on the floor, and sketch!" She makes art with her daughter regularly, exploring many different media and techniques. When asked how her art practice supports her life, she replied, "I know when it is missing!" When she is not making time for art in her life, she described being grumpy and irritable and that her family members will remind her to go and make art. Once in her studio, she enjoys making altered books which she described as "small, and containable. And I can close them back up." She also endorsed using other generative practices as a form of self-care like gardening and baking; these practices involve you in a multi-step process with a result in the end. Denise suggested that students begin during their training programs to develop "a sustainable habit of mind of self-care which includes art making." She also identified regular art practice as a way to continue to build empathy for what we ask our clients to do—the vulnerability of the art process.

Excuses
What excuses do you make to explain not picking up your instrument, sitting at your easel, or stepping on stage? Can you engage in the same levels of improvisation, flow, and play as you did when you were first honing your skills?

Excuses Self-talk _____
Fill a page with the excuses you make for not creating or engaging in an artistic practice of some kind. Once you have filled the speech bubbles, imagine the tone of voice, body language, and any other characteristics of each excuse. How might you respond with creativity to these voices?

Andra Duncan warned about giving in to your excuses:

> You don't have to deprive yourself of those things. If you're only working on music that is for your clients, you tend to lose your identity and that can lead to burnout. You've got to be able to separate and do things for yourself that are only for you.

As a helping professional, you need to take extra care that your identity as a helper does not keep you from helping yourself. Christine Hirabayashi identified going to museums as a way to refresh her artistic identity:

> I'm still figuring it out. But I try to give myself time. And if I'm not creative, really all I have to do is go visit an art museum and I'm right back in... If I don't have time to make art, I go see art.

She also said that she feels increasingly inspired by the local arts movement and makes time to attend the monthly arts events in her area. Do not let time and money be barriers—engaging in creative practices does not necessitate membership of the big museum or season tickets to the opera. Connect to local performance art organizations; make your commute an opportunity to immerse yourself in music you love; or pair your morning coffee with flipping through an art book or article about a new exhibition. Find ways to silence the excuses.

New techniques and technologies

An area of your earlier artistic life that may fall by the wayside in the pursuit of more practical or clinical training are the more technique-oriented areas. Realizing it had been years since I took a class with a pure technique focus, I walked back into the teaching studio of an undergraduate art professor for a three-day life drawing workshop. She had been one of my very favorite professors, so it was a joy to be in her classroom again. I knew my artist-self would benefit from the workshop, but I had not expected the other benefits. I was surprised by how widely applicable the experience was to so many aspects of my current work. Life drawing requires both close observation and a flowing, loose approach—traits I need to engage in the research and innovation work I do. I realized that life drawing necessitates maintaining an awareness about what is visible versus what I think or expect to see. Navigating this tension is excellent training for researchers. Being a learner again with no real risks was lovely; the experience met so many of my artistic and intellectual self-care needs. When the weekend was over, I made a promise to myself to explore ways to incorporate more formal artistic classes into my year.

Exploring new ideas and techniques for yourself also benefits your clients. As a clinician, you need to continue to challenge your skill and media comfort areas. Your ability to support your clients relies on your access to a wide range of media, techniques, styles, and approaches in your chosen art practice. I worked with a music therapist who, after consultation with the speech language therapist, taught herself to play the harmonica in order to facilitate a harmonica group with residents in skilled nursing that offered support for both their psychosocial and speech therapy goals. Ongoing artistic and technical development helps us better serve our clients.

Making time

Finding time to engage in your own creative practice is not always easy, particularly when balancing multiple jobs or competing priorities in personal and professional life. Newall wrote about her fears that the requirements of work might interrupt her creative growth:

> It has added increased stress to an already pressure-filled internship and graduate experience…however, I realize [that] without this added impetus to grow as an art therapist, I faced the likelihood of letting art making slip away into the default of becoming a counselor rather than an art therapist. I hear many similar concerns from other art therapy interns. (Junge & Newall, 2015, p. 110)

Creative practices in your workplaces can be a way to stay connected to your artistic self; Fahad al Fahed described having "time to work supporting students and teaching them" but less time available for his own visual art making. He teaches art and reads about art regularly, which keeps him connected to his artistic identity. Denise Wolf also endorsed the benefit of teaching in a studio-based program, where "art making is implicit in the teaching practices—so I'll make response art along with my students." Hadas Weissberg spoke about taking advantage of a dance class that was offered at the Jewish Community Center where she works as a way to address the lack of dance in her life, since she is in more of a management role and less of a therapeutic role. She expressed sadness about the decreased time to dance and was thinking about ways to prioritize it: "I'm thinking about it, thinking about how to open some groups for movement—things that are not therapeutic but that have the dance and movement as part of it—a group for women who want to dance." Making time for yourself might inspire others to make time alongside you.

Andra Duncan spoke about how she thinks about professional artistic access for music therapists—how they can engage in music without it being tied to clinical work:

I think being able to have your own things that you are able to listen to or work on. I didn't always have the luxury of this, but I would see it in the interns I worked with: being able to practice a piece they had worked on in college on piano. It was nothing they would incorporate therapeutically; they wouldn't play an entire Bach piece for their client. For them, they need it: it was part of their identity, that classical music piece. Being able to play on their instrument without having to constantly think about the therapeutic implications of it. Just doing it for themselves.

She talked about how interrelated her skill and passion as a vocalist are with her success as a clinician and her strategy for enjoying her "instrument" for her own benefit:

As a vocalist, I use my vocal skills to my benefit in session. I was classically trained and then trained in musical theater. Being able to get in the car and belt out a song that I just want to sing that was purely for myself. I don't have to think about who it is for. Even going to a concert or a musical—for me that really helps. Sometimes, I would just need to get away from the clients in the car or at home and listen to something that I like that was completely opposite of what I would ever play for clients. That would be what I would need sometimes—to separate.

Andra's words communicate how wide the arts are and how you can benefit from exploring styles and genres outside those you use with clients.

Making time to engage in your own creative growth will shift and change across your career. Christine Hirabayashi described using different artistic stimuli and opportunities at different times depending on her needs. Conversely, the form of your creative practice might be the constant in a life filled with change. I have kept art journals since I was 17 years old—this form has been with me through all my higher education and multiple cross-country moves. Changeable or static, staying attuned to your creative needs is important. Fatmah Al-Qadfan notices when she has not had enough time for creative pursuits:

I noticed that when I neglect my creative and artistic identity, I become lethargic and feel "stuck" at work. I try to lead improv workshops as an artist/director and not as a therapist. I wish I could direct a play, but for now I try to attend performances and concerts, and connect with other theater practitioners. I particularly enjoy attending rehearsals and witnessing a show come together. The possibilities are endless, and I tend to think outside the box in rehearsals.

She reflected on her experiences directing or assistant directing shows during graduate school, noting that it stimulated her cognition in a different way than her training to become a therapist, and that it was accessible: the theater was right next to where she was taking classes. Paying attention to how you feel when you do not have enough time to practice your art, and the benefits you feel when you do, can help to counteract some of those excuses you identified earlier.

 ## The Experience of Practicing _____

Think about how you feel when you practice your preferred art form. What sensations do you feel in your body? What emotion words would you associate with the practice?

Now think about how you feel when you do not make time to practice your preferred art form. What sensations do you feel in your body? What emotion words would you associate with not having time to practice?

Use your responses to these questions to guide your planning for the next month—how might you get your creative needs met?

___

Creative practices in research

Your own creative engagement can be part of how you conduct and understand research. Engaging in creative practices during your research, either as part of the methodology (Skains, 2018) or adjacent to the research, can help you see in new ways and stay open to potential findings: "If we judge too soon, we risk missing important information or inspiration from unanticipated sources" (Meier, Wegener, & Maslo,

2018, p. 3). Your artistic practice can help highlight and bring forward these pieces of information and create new knowledge. Creative practices and arts-based research use "art making as a tool for revealing ideas, understanding the world, and enabling us to know something that cannot be known in any other way" (Potash, 2019, p. 119) and creating the circumstances for resonance with the ideas being explored (Saratsi et al., 2019).

I utilized intentional art making as part of my research methods in two recent studies (Partridge, 2016b, 2019a, 2019d). The goal of the art practice was to bracket my bias as a researcher and assist in documenting the study progression. Engaging in self-reflexive practice has been recommended as a means to be more ethical and aware (Kapitan, 2015), as both a clinician and a researcher. It is a way to document "the detours in academic work that may originate from or spill over into our lives" (Meier et al., 2018, p. 3). You also need to consider how you structure your research in ways that privilege your own ways of knowing, sometimes unintentionally silencing the wisdom of your research participants (Guerin & Thain, 2018).

In the research collaboration described in Chapter 8, I kept an art journal for each day of the study. I made at least one entry a day with additional entries for unique situations I encountered. When the research concluded, I began a multi-step process of manipulating and continuing to work with the images, going back and forth between digital and traditional mark-making (Partridge, 2019d). In a previous study, I completed one image following the same protocol the participants did for every interaction with a participant in the study (Partridge, 2016b). In both cases, the process of creating and later reflecting on the images deepened my understanding of the methods, data, and analysis.

For students in my thesis class, we use art prompts to explore their research ideas and their emotional experience around doing research. Engaging in this process enables us to have conversations about both their own experiences as new researchers as well as to practice looking at a "data set" of art created from a shared prompt each week. Research can feel like a far-off task, especially for students or for clinicians who have been removed from academic contexts for years, but there are many ways you might be able to get involved in research or begin a study of your own (Kremer et al., 2016, 2017). You have expertise that can benefit the field and the clients you serve.

 If you are considering engaging in program evaluation or formal research studies, consider how you might incorporate your creative practices into the methods or into your analysis.

Art practice evolving over time

As we progress in our careers, age, and eventually move towards retirement, our artist-self matures and may face functional challenges. I recently spoke with a retired art therapist who expressed sadness about the change in her ability due to arthritis. She seemed a little hesitant to apply to her own art practice any skills at adaptation. We talked through some possible modifications she could make, and she recalled making these adaptations for her clients, but was hesitant about doing that for herself. This reaction may be connected to other problematic assumptions and behaviors about clients' use of materials and practitioners giving themselves time and space to create (Partridge, 2016a). Having an openness to the ways your own practices will change is important.

Donna Newman-Bluestein had some recommendations for how to take care of yourself as a clinician in the arts therapies: "I think most important is having an attitude of self-love, self-care, and forgiveness. Gentleness. Because if that's not there, it won't work. It has to come out of a genuine, internal desire or need." Part of this "gentleness" is, as several contributors described, letting your creative practice evolve and making time and space for it in your life. Engaging in creative work of some kind and staying connected with your identity as an artist are important for your longevity in the field. It will also infuse your work with clients with a deeper connection to the techniques and practices you bring into sessions.

CHAPTER 10

Leaving a Trace

This chapter covers strategies and approaches to ensuring longevity of creative arts therapies in your setting—ensuring that one person leaving a position does not mean elimination of the creative arts therapy service entirely. Many of us are the first to work in our setting and hope to not be the last. This chapter includes discussion of developing the field through mentoring students, creating training programs, engaging in inquiry, and publishing about research and practice.

Leaving a trace can happen many different ways; with forethought and planning, you can shape the future of creative arts therapy in your work settings and across your communities. Over the course of our interview, Denise Wolf spoke about the large and small ways she creates space for others in the field. One way she thinks about contributing to the future of art therapy is by serving in various professional capacities. She described her work as "continuing the process of art therapy to be an understood and respected field." Kari Rogenski also spoke about service at the national level to support and promote drama therapy, as covered in Chapter 5.

Mentoring curious students

My early experiences of access to the field of art therapy via an artist-in-residence position cemented in my mind and heart the importance of being open and available to curious students, new professionals, and those in allied fields. Having the opportunity to meet and work alongside an art therapist helped confirm my interest in pursuing a degree in the field. Since becoming an art therapist myself, I have hosted many high school students and undergraduate students interested in art therapy. This work has included sitting for interviews, arranging for student shadow days when appropriate and ethically possible, or consulting on their class assignments. It is very rewarding to provide for those students something I myself did not have access to.

 Many contributors to this book described finding out about their field by accident or happenstance.

How might you help more people get exposed to your creative arts therapy discipline?

What can you do to address the lack of information?

One strategy is to consider the mentoring of students and support for new professionals as part of the service to your profession.

Jess Minckley created an image (Figure 10.1) to illustrate the frustration that can come up when you want to understand the world you are entering, but come up against barriers to accessing the information. Her work is about "the inaccessibility of information about the art therapy profession." She commented:

> It seems difficult to apprehend answers about the practical reality of art therapy as a profession when you're unaffiliated with an institution. Once inside an institution, there are gatekeeping practices that can potentially have adverse repercussions for students, which revokes personal agency.

Christine Hirabayashi echoed this image's themes as she remembered calls that went unanswered when she was trying to find out information about the field of art therapy and wanted to talk with someone in the field about what to expect.

Donna Newman-Bluestein spoke about the first dance therapist she met, and the impact that conversation had on her path: "Everything she recommended, whether it was reading or people to meet or study with, I followed." She said that following the recommendations of this first dance therapist gave her a great deal of inspiration and guided her on her path towards entering the field herself. Once you've followed the advice and guidance and become a creative arts therapist, you might think about ways to give the gift of mentorship to someone else.

Figure 10.1 "Ivory Tower"—digital drawing by Jess Minckley

✎ Gatekeeper Exercise _____

Where do you function as a gatekeeper?

. . . .

. . . .

. . . .

Do you have information that people considering entering the field would find valuable?

. . . .

. . . .

. . . .

How might you see your role as an opportunity to make space for others?

. . . .

. . . .

. . . .

Having an open-door policy to students can also provide opportunities to advocate for your field. When an undergraduate student approached the nonprofit where I work about conducting his capstone research in our community, he originally labeled what he would be doing with older adults as music therapy, though he was not a music therapy student and was not supervised under a music therapist. It was not necessarily the student's fault—he was attending a school without a music therapy program and perhaps his advising professor did not know any better. I worked with him on his application for study with the university's institutional review board and educated him about use of the term "music therapy" along with several other forms of problematic language in his initial proposal document. Had we not made space for his project in our community, his proposal might have gone forward without checking that language, resulting in perpetuating confusion about the creative arts therapies.

Christine Hirabayashi also sees working with students who are interested in the arts as part of her role, and uses it as an opportunity to educate and advocate by "always making sure we talk about the field and the profession and what it is. And the requirements." She spoke about how rewarding it can be to see students find out about the field and get excited. Relevant to the concerns raised in Jess Minckley's art, she also makes sure to give them a realistic picture of what it will take to become an art therapist: graduate study, accrual of hours towards licensure, board certification, testing, and thesis-writing. She used her own experiences with all the requirements as an example: "I am careful about it. Because if you bombard a person with that, it will feel like, 'I will never be able to do it.' But I do tell them about it because it's the realistic picture." She balances discussion of all the hoops to jump through with some discussion about how rewarding she finds the work and how much she loves what she does each day.

Because he lectures in the art education department at his university, Fahad al Fahed has the opportunity to share about art therapy with his students. For some, he is their first point of contact in the field: "A lot of them get interested in art therapy. They ask questions and try to access resources." One barrier his students face is that there are few books on art therapy in Arabic and no official training to become art therapists in Saudi Arabia yet. He is able to provide resources about short trainings so they can find out more. He said that he does not "just explain" but rather uses their art as a means to explore the psychological elements of art making; his students have a lived experience of using their art. I follow this same approach when working with high school or undergraduate students—not teaching technique but rather enabling their own self-exploration. This embodied learning serves as a powerful introduction to the work you do.

 Imagined Student _____

Imagine a student contacts you to find out about the work you do. Do some writing to work through how you'll respond.

How can you invite students into your creative arts therapy world?

What are the high and low points you would share with them?

What resources would you recommend they look into?

What follow-up would you offer to them?

....

....

....

Stigma reduction

Working with students is also an opportunity to engage in advocacy about the issues your clients experience, including stigma about seeking mental health treatment. Given the damaging impact of mental health stigma, especially in the ways it limits community connectedness and social networks (Howells & Zelnik, 2009), bringing students into your clinical and community creative-arts-therapy worlds can have far-reaching impacts. In my work, exposing students to the rewarding nature of work with older adults has given me the opportunity to educate about ageism along with art therapy. I wrote about several of these initiatives in my first book (Partridge, 2019c), and have continued to expand this work. The nonprofit where I work has a summer internship program for college students, where our primary objective is to use the internship as a means to further our anti-ageism work. We also serve as an internship and practicum placement site for students from different disciplines from several universities, including public health, nursing, and design. Hosting students has been mutually beneficial—we provide education and experience and we learn along with them as they complete projects and explore cutting edge ideas.

Both/and: Artist and therapist

Your work in the creative arts therapies necessitates some discussion of other arts careers. Each of the creative arts therapies has a connection to the fine and performing arts—worlds that are very different from the world of therapy and therapists. You can assist students in finding the right path for themselves in the arts, whether that be in the arts therapies or in other sectors of creative work.

Tawanna Benbow encourages young people she meets to follow their passion into acting when they feel called to be a working actor, a role she makes sure she differentiates from being a "celebrity." She reported doing some serious reality checks with them about the difficulties and joys of life in the performing arts. Choosing the creative arts therapy path does not require removing yourself from the fine and performing art world. You can also model participation in the arts beyond your therapeutic work—exhibiting in art shows, singing in community choirs, and performing with regional groups. As described in Chapter 8, Fatmah Al-Qadfan was able to combine her expertise in drama therapy with her interest in participating in productions—look for opportunities that grant you access to parts of the arts you do not often encounter in the therapy session.

Mentoring new professionals

Many credentialing processes have some mentoring built in through required supervision. Junge defined mentoring as a more flexible, mutual process: "The new art therapist evolves more quickly through the wisdom of the more experienced guide. Both grow from their different vantage points" (Junge & Newall, 2015, p. 101). This mutually beneficial approach to supervision and mentorship can create a very fulfilling relationship.

We can also mentor and receive mentorship in less formal ways. Stromstead (2001) wrote about the benefit of talking with people who came before her in the dance therapy lineage for a research study; she endeavored "to dialogue with women who represented the next phase in my own journey: mature practitioners, whose lives had been irrevocably changed by their movement practice" (p. 39). The internet and the proliferation of easier access to the means of sharing media creates new forms of mentorship. Two of my former students started a podcast in order to "interview a variety of art therapists to build community, share knowledge, and join in the efforts to bring art therapy into the digital age" (Cody & Winslow, 2019). Their efforts enable their own exploration and mentorship as well as that of their listening audience.

Denise Wolf spoke about her approach to teaching and mentoring that involves a great deal of modeling healthy, adaptive responses to mistakes: "I have to be careful," she joked, "because I don't want them to see me as wildly incompetent, but I am mindful that I share stories where things go wrong or things go super-sideways." She then encourages looking for the useful or informative content to be learned from the difficult situation—she called it "loving the dandelions." She shares these stories with her mentees not just as examples, but to show them that it is safe for them to share their fears, mistakes, and difficulties. She affirms their sharing with genuine gratitude and recognizes how difficult it can be to share in that way. You will benefit immensely from mentorship opportunities across your work trajectory: you have so many chances to learn on both sides of the relationship.

Mentorship Relationship Gives and Gets _____

Make a list in two columns. On one side, write what you need, want, and expect from a mentorship relationship. On the other side, write what you provide, offer, and give.

....

....

....

....

....

....

Notice which side is longer or seems to contain more.

How could you even it out?

Hint: Sometimes you might seek in a mentor what is more appropriate for therapy. Or you might be fearful or ashamed to ask for what you really need.

_____

_____

 Considering the two lists you made, make an image or other creative expression representing a healthy, thriving mentorship relationship.

_____

Thirst for knowledge

Part of ensuring your longevity in the field and the continued develop-ment of your practices, programs, and scholarship necessitates ongoing inquiry. Tapping into the curiosity you possess is a way to stay engaged with your work and your career. Newall wrote that the mentoring relationship she had with Junge was part of sating this thirst for knowledge: "I've had the experience to think about what I'm doing. Mentorship is one way—especially after graduation—that I can continue to keep creating the conditions to learn" (Junge & Newall, 2015, p. 107). Other learning opportunities might include training in sub-specialties or additional certifications.

 Drinking Glass Prompt _____

How do you sate your thirst for knowledge? What fills this glass up?

You might explore doing this directive several ways:

- Use line, shape, and color to fill the glass with a representation of different ways you stimulate your own creativity and interest in learning.

- Use collaged or written words and phrases to fill the cup.

- Take a chronological approach; start by representing learning and knowledge acquisition you've done so far and then project into the future with your ideas for how you'll continue to fill your cup.

- You could use this prompt on a regular basis as a weekly/monthly/quarterly check-in.

Supporting your thirst for knowledge can also come through self-directed readings. As discussed in Chapter 1, scheduling time for reading is a great way to ensure you make time for your own intellectual stimulation. The graphic medicine list (Appendix 3) is a good jumping-off point! Attend lectures in your community. Share ideas and inspiration with others.

Read the literature from your own discipline, but also papers and books from allied fields and from fields far different than your own.

Position relay

One strategy to ensure a position stays open to creative arts therapists is to hand it off directly to a supervisee ready to move up. Particularly if you have worked hard to create a dynamic role for yourself as a creative arts therapist, you will want to ensure that role stays filled by someone who can build upon your work.

Though my new position is primarily based in the support center, I regularly check in with and have groups with the older adults at the community where I used to work full-time. Recently, one older adult expressed the change she noticed since I was no longer in the building every day. I asked her about the quality of her relationships and she replied, "It was better during the time that you were here because there were more people I could get near to. Now I stay inside. I love the outside, but I need others to want the same thing." She went on to say she feels less opportunity to connect with her peers. Though it feels nice to have made an impact, her words reveal what can happen when you do not ensure a continuity of care—something we spend more time thinking about in private practice than in community settings. I am working on addressing the lack of an art therapist at the systems level, as described in Chapter 5.

Keeping the Path Clear

Return to the trailblazing directive from Chapter 1 as a stimulus to write about keeping the path clear for others. Consider the following questions:

How do you keep the path clear for those who follow in your footsteps?

What maps or markers do you have to leave out for those who come down the path later?

How can you help them avoid some of the difficulties you encountered?

Are there any lessons you believe they need to learn through experience?

How do your clients contribute to a continued path for a creative arts therapist in your setting?

....

....

....

....

....

....

....

Research and inquiry

Research and program evaluation are important ways to inform your own practice and contribute to the field. It is part of how you can help your discipline and the creative arts therapies grow, continue to evolve, and extend into new areas. Your efforts to evaluate your work will help you and your coworkers improve the practices you implement with clients: presenting and publishing about the experience can help others avoid your mistakes, amplify your successes, and ultimately better serve more clients. If you are engaged in innovative work with clients, conducting research and publishing it can be a way to ensure the work extends beyond the walls of your own setting and impacts greater numbers of clients.

In a letter to future art therapists, Frances Kaplan had the following advice about research: "Encourage research, do research, and keep up with the research in art therapy and related fields" (Junge & Newall, 2015, p. 127). How do you get involved in research if it has not been part of your practice? One great place to start is to regularly read the foundational and emerging research in your field or related to the population you work with. It is also important to recognize your fears about engaging in research:

> We know that research is hard. And captivating, infuriating, rewarding, and addictive. It can be daunting, too, for new researchers. Much of "how" to go about the act of research is unspoken. Methods may be explicit, but they don't deal with the detail of what to actually do when things go wrong or with our own reactions to the process—especially the emotional ones. (Williams, Jones, & Robertson, 2014, p. 2)

To address these fears, read more research. As you read, think about how you would do things differently if it was your study or how you might apply the methodologies in your setting or area of interest. Explore research from diverse fields. Participate in other people's research (especially student projects—they need you!). Take some of the fear away through exposure.

Read more research in your field. Explore research that uses interesting or innovative methodologies. When you find a study you especially like, explore the works the authors cite in their reference list.

Rejection

In your efforts to "leave a trace" through presentation, publication, and other means of bringing your work to new audiences, you will certainly experience some rejections. Unfortunately, there is no secret antidote to rejection or fail-proof tip to win every grant you apply for. But that does not mean you should not try. Rejection is part of seeking publication, submitting conference proposals, and seeking funding or support for new opportunities. As mentioned in the introduction, most of us are far more comfortable celebrating wins rather than speaking aloud about rejection. Submitting scholarly work for peer review is "a symbolic interaction that is goal-relevant for individual scholars" (Horn, 2016, p. 14) and has implications for your personal and professional identities.

There are many barriers to publication (Hyland, 2016) and acceptance to present at conferences. One area of stress can come from the variability in peer-review rigor, processes, and timelines (Hargens, 1990). Stress from rejection may be exacerbated by your discomfort with talking about rejection. The more you avoid it or think about rejection as a secret to hide, the higher your stress levels about the current and future rejections. These fears can get in the way of your seeking out a grant funding or speaking to a potential supporter who could help you with the next step you want to take in your career. Do not let the sting of the rejection prevent you from learning from the experience. Ask the granting organization for feedback, and read and consider the peer-reviewer's comments; you may not agree with all the feedback, but it can be really constructive and can inform your next submission. The best advice to counter this fear is to take a deep breath and click the submit button, ask for the support, and apply for the funding—just try! And when you do encounter rejection, talk about it.

As a creative arts therapist, you have some additional tools for exploring your responses to rejection. You can create images, music, movement, or dramatic responses to the emotions you feel; you can perform the words of the rejection aloud to take the sting out; and you can cut and paste the pieces of the review you want to hold on to as opportunities for growth. Rejections are neither all good nor all bad: "Peer rejections offer the chance for personal enhancement; but they also potentially discredit scholarly integrity" (Horn, 2016, p. 14). The way you respond to rejection will influence how you move forward.

Responding to Rejection _____

Think about how you have responded to rejection in the past.

What were your emotional responses?

How did you behave?

What was your posture or facial expression like in the moment?

Were you able to find learning opportunities in the rejection? What were they?

Did you talk about it with anyone else? Why or why not?

What longer-term impacts did the rejection have on your behavior?

_____

Do not let fear of rejection keep you from submitting proposals for conferences, applying for jobs, seeking promotions, or writing and submitting articles to journals! Your knowledge and experience are important. Likewise, do not hold rejections close to your chest in shame. The more you are able to talk about your experiences of rejection, the more resilient the whole field will become. Recently, I saw a scholar in art therapy I really admire post about her research team's successes and rejections in the same post. It really helped to put into context the success I witnessed from the outside. It also prompted me to pick myself up out of a slump I was in after two rejections in the same week—one of a paper and one of a presentation submission. Sharing the whole picture of your career, success and struggle, can have a positive impact on others. Sometimes the trace we leave is through our brave honesty about difficult experiences.

On becoming

Perhaps a more accurate title for this chapter is "Leaving Traces," since you are likely to make your mark in many different ways across the course of your career. As evidenced by the experiences and stories shared in this book, the path to becoming a creative arts therapist looks different for everyone, and invites you to grow and develop in many different ways. Your professional identity will continue to evolve over time: "There's no limit," Kari Rogenski exclaimed. Creative arts therapists are engaged in work that ranges from traditional individual therapy to work at the community and systems level. There are some things along the path that you will share with other creative arts therapists, as Fatmah Al-Qadfan said: "No matter where we are in the world, creative arts therapists have these parallel stories and experiences." She mentioned that she found these parallel experiences comforting, having studied in the US and now living in Kuwait. As Christine Hirabayashi stated "everyone has their own life path, because I did a lot of things in-between." She advocates for sharing about the realities of your journeys into your career as both a form of inspiration as well as a balanced representation of what to expect. I hope this book becomes another comforting reminder as you move through your career and leave your mark in small and large ways on the field of creative arts therapy. Just as the stories in this book inspire and inform your evolution, your process of becoming can leave a trace by helping others see a path forward—so share it! Your career joins with others to build the legacy of the field.

To conclude, I hope this book inspires you to collaborate with and support your creative arts therapy peers. Jess Minckley created a hopeful image about interdisciplinary collaboration (Figure 10.2). Her words about the work are a powerful closure to your journey through this book and out into the world:

> We strengthen our sense of self and simultaneously our professional identities by working with one another as part of a bigger whole. I get to share intimacy being in-relationship with people in this discipline. I get to meet amazing people in art therapy, which is truly a gift. I know art therapists all over this country and in Canada. Feeling part of a larger community helps us do better research, and working alongside one another allows us to gain a more complex understanding of theoretical applications and the ideology behind our work. And we can ask for help and feedback so we can grow personally and professionally.

Figure 10.2 "Together"—digital drawing by Jess Minckley

Contributor Biographies

Fahad al Fahed will help you learn to use language appropriate to your audience.

Fahad al Fahed is from Saudi Arabia with a lifelong interest in art. He has studied art and art therapy both in Saudi Arabia and the United States, studying art education at King Saud University, which is where he found out about the field of art therapy. He studied under Dr. Alyami, the first person to be credentialed as an art therapist in Saudi Arabia. While working on his first master's degree in art education and teaching in the university's art education department, Fahad completed a thesis on art therapy in spinal rehabilitation. He continued to pursue education in art therapy—first with a master's degree from NYU and later a Ph.D in art therapy from Notre Dame de Namur University in California. He is actively working to establish art therapy in Saudi Arabia.

Fatmah Al-Qadfan will help you learn to advocate for yourself and your profession.

Fatmah Al-Qadfan is the first Registered Drama Therapist (RDT) in her home country, Kuwait. She received her master's and training at Kansas State University and holds a postgraduate certificate in post-traumatic stress studies. Previously she taught Arabic on a Fulbright Teaching assistantship at Jackson State University in Mississippi. Fatmah enjoys weaving the expressive arts into her work, whether she is facilitating workshops in the community or at a school, or seeing clients at the clinic. She primarily works with individuals recovering from complex trauma and eating disorders. Fatmah utilizes drama therapy to increase connection and awareness of the body, to expand the range of emotional expression, and to help people experience catharsis.

Tawanna Benbow will help you see how your work connects to the greater community.

Tawanna Benbow is a thespian, mythologist, and cultivator of people. She is a doctoral candidate in mythological studies with an emphasis in depth psychology at Pacifica Graduate Institute (Santa Barbara, California), and is currently working on her production style dissertation *Sanctified Passion: A Mythodrama of Mary Magdalene*. She has obtained her master's in the dual degree program; her Master of Arts in Theology with an emphasis in theology and arts from Fuller Theological Seminary (California); her Master of Fine Arts (MFA) in acting from the University of Missouri–Kansas City; her Bachelor of Fine Arts (BFA) with a concentration in acting/directing from North Carolina A&T State University; and she is currently becoming a Registered Drama Therapist (RDT) with the North American Drama Therapy Association.

She has lived in New York, where she pursued her acting career prior to relocating to Los Angeles. Tawanna has film and television credits and has acted in numerous plays and performed at several regional theater companies. She is creating a new approach to contribute to the field of dramatherapy called *mythodrama*. Her therapeutic methodology uses theology, mythology, depth psychology, and theater as a collective means to aid in this unique process. Tawanna has a dedication to people and a passion to see souls healed and whole: that no one should walk around wounded or with trauma, and that everyone's personal narrative can be modified—reflected upon, reclaimed, and rewritten! She works with the idea brought forward by Maya Angelou—*"There is no greater agony than bearing an untold story inside you."*

Andra Duncan will help you to own your role as a leader in an interdisciplinary team.

Andra Duncan has been a board-certified music therapist since 2010. She completed her bachelor's degree in music performance, with an emphasis in musical theater, from Ouachita Baptist University in Arkansas. During her senior year at OBU, Andra studied abroad for a semester at Salzburg College in Austria. She completed her music therapy equivalency at the University of the Pacific in California, and is presently a candidate to complete her thesis for the MA in music therapy from UOP.

After completing her music therapy internship at the Exempla Colorado Lutheran Home, a residential care community for elders in Colorado, Andra began her career and worked for four years at Elder Care Alliance communities within the San Francisco Bay Area of California. She specializes in music therapy in geriatrics, is a Certified Eden Alternative Associate, and is certified in the "I'm Still Here" approach to memory care. Additionally, Andra has almost five years of experience working with individuals of all ages with neurodevelopmental disabilities, psychiatric disorders, and learning disabilities in Chicago and Indianapolis. She is a Certified Laughter Yoga Leader and enjoys incorporating laughter into her music therapy sessions whenever appropriate.

Christine Hirabayashi will help you seek the mentorship you need in your workplace.

Christine Hirabayashi, Ph.D, LMFT, ATR-BC is a Licensed Marriage and Family Therapist, Board Certified Art Therapist, and Doctorate of Philosophy in art therapy. She received her Bachelor of Fine Arts degree in illustration from California State University, Long Beach and subsequently her master's degree in marriage and family therapy and art therapy from Notre Dame de Namur University in California. She received her Doctorate of Philosophy in art therapy at NDNU. Christine's early clinical experience includes working in hospice care with terminally ill patients and bereaved family members. She conducted group and individual therapy for children and adults using art therapy as a compassionate way to process difficult feelings around grief and loss.

Since 2004, Christine has specialized in chronic pain management; she works for an interdisciplinary Functional Restoration Program (FRP) and Trauma Rehabilitation Program (TRP) at Integrated Pain Management Medical Group in Northern California. At IPM Medical Group, she also provides individual art therapy, art therapy support groups, and workshops, and facilitates an offsite open art studio that fosters a supportive community and ongoing creative outlet for those who have chronic pain.

In private practice, Christine offers psychotherapy and art therapy to adults and teens struggling with depression, anxiety, chronic pain, trauma, medical conditions, grief/loss, and life transitions, which include work, family, and relationship issues. With her passion for helping others express emotion through art, her vision is to continue finding innovative ways to strengthen and heal the mind and body through the use of art therapy.

Coleen Lorenz will help you reconnect with the work you really want to do in service of the community you want to support.
Collen Lorenz, BC-DMT, CGP, HeartMath Resilience Advantage Trainer, and Reiki Master, is a movement therapist specializing in body, mind, and heart integration for personalized growth and self-empowerment. Coleen is the founder of Arts Unity Movement and Artistic Director of NewGround Theatre Dance Company. She has served on the faculty at Notre Dame de Namur University (California) and Notre Dame High School, teaching psychology and dance.

Donna Newman-Bluestein will help you learn to trust the process and try things out.
Donna Newman-Bluestein, BC-DMT, CMA, LMHC is a board-certified dance/movement therapist, Certified Movement Analyst, mental health counselor, and performer with intergenerational dance company Back Pocket Dancers. Since receiving her M.Ed in expressive therapies with a major in dance/movement therapy from Lesley University (Massachusetts). She has worked with children with physical disabilities, adults in acute psychiatric distress and in medical rehabilitation, and senior adults in long-term care and assisted-living residences. As an educator, supervisor, international trainer, and speaker, Donna's work for the past 15 years has focused entirely on transforming the culture of care for people with dementia through dance and embodied caregiving. She has co-authored numerous professional articles and published a train-the-trainer manual, *The Dance of Interaction: Nonverbal Communication Training for Caregivers of People with Dementia, An Embodied Approach.* To motivate people to engage through movement, she created the Octaband, a tool to foster

a sense of connection through movement. The Octaband and other products she designed are useful for people of all ages.

Jess Minckley will help you learn to advocate for yourself and ask important questions.
Jess Minckley is a graduate student in the Clinical Mental Health Counseling and Art Therapy program at Antioch University Seattle. Prior to pursuing graduate training in art therapy, she taught at the college level and continues to have an interest in pedagogy. Jess holds a BFA and MFA from Otis College of Art and Design, Los Angeles; She is an illustrator and owner of minc.work, a dog fanatic, and Adlerian open to creative collaborations.

Kari Rogenski will help you identify ways to collaborate towards successes.
Kari Rogenski, RDT, LMFT has a love of elders that began as a child, and spending time with her three grandmothers was always a joy. Grandma's house was always her favorite place to be.

Kari combined her passion for eldercare and the creative arts by becoming a Licensed Marriage and Family Therapist and Registered Drama Therapist working with elders. She brings over ten years of experience to her role as Director of the Hummingbird Project and co-creator of Joyful Moments: Meaningful Activities to Engage Older Adults, and is a proud advocate for the importance of finding and embracing joy throughout life. She has presented to both professional and public audiences locally and nationally about quality of life and life enrichment for older and disabled adults, including several presentations for the Alzheimer's Association, the Aging Life Care Professional Association, and the North American Drama Therapy Association, among others.

It is Kari's creative and professional approach, as well as her warm personality, that allows her to connect with clients and engage them in meaningful therapeutic activities. Kari's passion for theater has been infused into her education and career. She has expertise in facilitating drama therapy techniques including improvisation, monologue writing, and play reading. Some of her favorite activities to share with older adults include expressive arts such as life story collage, art appreciation, touch drawing, creative storytelling, legacy projects, and more.

Kari serves on the board of directors of the North American Drama Therapy Association where she plays an integral role in promoting the profession of drama therapy in both the United States and Canada. She is also honored to serve as treasurer of Creative Aging San Francisco, a collective of creative aging professionals serving Bay Area elders. Kari is Clinical MFT Supervisor for the San Francisco Campus for Jewish Living where she works closely to train future drama and creative arts therapists in eldercare. She is currently pursuing her Ph.D in psychology with a specialization in creativity studies at Saybrook University, California.

Hadas Weissberg will help you learn to follow where your career path leads you.
Hadas Weissberg is a dance and movement therapist, and has a Ph.D in expressive therapy from Lesley University, Massachusetts. She is a creative program manager with over 15 years of experience initiating, leading, and running programs and events focusing on community growth and engagement. Hadas is passionate about developing strong communities and making a difference in individuals' lives by executing ideas and vision. She is the Kids, Youth and Families Program Manager at the Oshman Family Jewish Community Center.

Denise Wolf will help you learn to be brave as you evolve into your professional role.
Denise Wolf has worked with children, adolescents, and families for over 15 years, guiding clients on courageous journeys. She began as Assistant Director at Cedar Crest College in Pennsylvania in August of 2019, teaching in both the graduate and undergraduate programs. Prior to her position at Cedar Crest she was an adjunct professor at Drexel University (in Philadelphia) in the Art Therapy and Counseling graduate program, in the undergraduate Art Therapy Concentration program at the University of the Arts, in the Community Trauma and Counseling Graduate program, Art Therapy Specialization, at Jefferson University, and in the Master in Counseling program at Villanova University in Pennsylvania.

Denise holds an MA in art therapy, is a Registered, Board Certified Art Therapist as well as an Art Therapy Credentialed Supervisor (ATCS), and is a Licensed Professional Counselor. She is an active member of many professional associations including the American Art Therapy Association, and the Delaware Valley Art Therapy Association, Specialists of Schools, and is a working board member of the Accreditation Council for Art Therapy Education. Denise has presented at many national conferences about the intersection of art therapy, neurobiology, and trauma-informed care.

Denise maintains an active clinical practice in her private work, Mangata Services, treating children, adolescents, and families who have experienced trauma and grief. Through her practice she works as a consultant for a residential treatment facility for adolescents providing dialectical behavior therapy (DBT) training and skills groups, as a trauma-informed education trainer for the Philadelphia Art Museum, and as a clinical group supervision facilitator for Mastery Charter Schools.

Recent professional contributions include publication of a chapter titled, "Adolescent Group Art Therapy" in *Creative Arts-Based Group Therapy with Adolescents: Theory and Practice*, edited by C. Haen and N. Boyd Webb. In April 2019 she facilitated an art experiential at the Third Annual Survivor-Led Symposium Survivor Retreat, "Engaging Survivors of Commercial Sexual Exploitation to End Gender-Based Violence," at Villanova University, Pennsylvania, where she was aided by one of her current graduate art therapy students. Denise also presented at the Jefferson Trauma Training Network (J-TEN), a four-hour NBCC-credited workshop titled "Trauma, Neurobiology and Sensory Interventions I" in November of 2018. She recently presented at the British Association of Art Therapists International Art Therapy Practice/Research Conference in London, as well as at the American Art Therapy Association Annual Conference in Kansas City.

Everyone Starts Somewhere

Humans are innately creative. But we often shut ourselves down from tapping into our creativity or resist the word itself because we tie it so closely to art with a capital A.

Part of our role is shifting both our internal thinking (how we plan, how we approach, and how we evaluate) and our external behavior (how we LIVE this out in words/actions/practice with the older adults we work with).

The end-goal is not necessarily that each of our communities is filled with late-life artistic bloomers; the goal is to transform our practice from delivering programming, towards spontaneous, creative, dynamic engagement.

Approaches:
Respond in-the-moment to resident questions and curiosity.

Encourage safe rule-breaking, especially in the protection of dignity. *Example*: If a game is too difficult for someone's cognitive function, make up a new game. Or use the game in a different manner. Or if residents are fixated on "crafts," encourage them to use the craft kit in a new and innovative way. This will require that you MODEL this behavior!

Bring in links to known interests and passions.

Take this approach to ALL you do.

Model the joy of spontaneity: if you have fun, your staff learns it is okay to have fun too…and all of this translates directly to resident joy.

Things to expect:
There will be resistance. Some folks will come and expect to be performed to. Don't give up! Find an ally in the room and invite them into your creative space.

Culture-change movements do not happen overnight and they do not follow a set trajectory. Unfortunately, I cannot provide a step-by-step system for implementing change.

Expect empowerment.

Expect laughter and other evidence of strong feelings!

Expect to get TIRED, but in a *good* way.

Graphic Medicine Titles for Therapists

With all these graphic novel and comic recommendations, please read/ view the content yourself prior to recommending them to clients. Some of the content and imagery may be distressing to clients, especially if they are viewing it at home or on their own. Always consider safety and suitability before making a recommendation.

Chast, R. (2014). *Can't we talk about something more pleasant?* Bloomsbury.
This book deals with issues related to aging, familial care provision, grief, death, and changing family dynamics. Sometimes humorous, sometimes heart-rending, the book does an excellent job of illustrating the experience of interacting with aging family members.

Cunningham, D. (2013). *Psychiatric tales*. Blank Slate.
The chapters of this book each portray a different mental health concern, including that of the author. This book directly addresses the stigma people living with mental illness face, and is an excellent read for students and new professionals as well as a potential resource for psychoeducation.

Forney, E. (2012). *Marbles: Mania, depression, Michelangelo, and me.* Gotham.
A graphic memoir covering the creator's experiences of treatment for bipolar disorder and how that treatment impacted her life and creative pursuits.

Green, K. (2017). *Lighter than my shadow*. Oni Press.
This book deals with issues of eating disorders, abuse, and recovery.

Haines, S. (2016). *Trauma is really strange*. Singing Dragon.
Accessible and dynamic exploration of the science, treatment, and lived experience of trauma. Part of a series that also covers pain and anxiety. All three are a must-have for the therapist's bookshelf or for waiting-room reading.

Penfold, R. (2006). *Dragonslippers: This is what an abusive relationship looks like*. Black Cat/Grove Press.
This book tells the story of the entire trajectory of an abusive relationship. Would be an excellent resource for someone who has experienced intimate partner violence as well as for family or friends wanting to better understand and support someone in or leaving an abusive relationship.

Perry, P. (2010). *Couch fiction: A graphic tale of psychotherapy*. Palgrave Macmillan.
Excellent resource for aspiring or new therapists, this book demonstrates some of the inner workings of therapy.

Stoian, M. (2016). *Take it as a compliment*. Singing Dragon.
The artist illustrates different people's experiences of harassment, abuse, and violence. Powerful for psychoeducation, awareness-raising, and empathy-building.

Walker, T. O. (2017). *Not my shame*. Singing Dragon.
Powerful work from the point of view of an adult survivor of childhood sexual abuse.

References

Allen, P. B. (1995). *Art is a way of knowing*. Shambhala.

Barry, P., & O'Callaghan, C. (2008). Reflexive journal writing. *Nordic Journal of Music Therapy, 17*(1), 55–66. doi:10.1080/08098130809478196

Carolan, R. (2001). Models and paradigms of art therapy research. *Art Therapy, 18*(4), 190–206. doi:10.1080/07421656.2001.10129537

Chilton, G., Gerity, L., LaVorgna-Smith, M., & MacMichael, H. N. (2009). An online art exchange group: 14 secrets for a happy artist's life. *Art Therapy, 26*(2), 66–72. doi:10.10 80/07421656.2009.10129741

Cody, J., & Winslow, L. (2019). Art therapy decoded. https://art-therapy-decoded.simplecast. com

Covey, S. R. (1989). *The 7 habits of highly effective people*. Free Press.

Curtis, S. L. (2012). Music therapy and social justice: A personal journey. *Arts in Psychotherapy, 39*(3), 209–213. doi:/10.1016/j.aip.2011.12.004

de Jonge, J., Shimazu, A., & Dollard, M. (2018). Short-term and long-term effects of off-job activities on recovery and sleep: A two-wave panel study among health care employees. *International Journal of Environmental Research and Public Health, 15*(9), 1–11. doi:10.3390/ijerph15092044

Digiuni, M., Jones, F. W., & Camic, P. M. (2013). Perceived social stigma and attitudes towards seeking therapy in training: A cross-national study. *Psychotherapy, 50*(2), 213–223. doi:10.1037/a0028784

Dissanayake, E. (1995). *Homo aestheticus: Where art comes from and why*. University of Washington Press.

Edwards, D. (2004). *Art therapy*. Sage Publications.

Ettarh, F. M. (2017, May 30). Vocational Awe? [Blog post] *WTF Is a Radical Librarian, Anyway?* https://fobaziettarh.wordpress.com/2017/05/30/vocational-awe

Ettarh, F. M. (2018). Vocational awe and librarianship: The lies we tell ourselves. *In the Library with the Lead Pipe*. www.inthelibrarywiththeleadpipe.org/2018/vocational-awe

Fosslien, L., & Duffy, M. W. (2019). *No hard feelings: The secret power of embracing emotions at work*. Portfolio/Penguin.

Gardstrom, S. C., & Jackson, N. A. J. (2011). Personal therapy for undergraduate music therapy students: A survey of AMTA program coordinators. *Journal of Music Therapy, 48*(2), 226–255. doi:10.1093/jmt/48.2.226

Garvey, E. G. (2013). *Writing with scissors: American scrapbooks from the Civil War to the Harlem Renaissance*. Oxford University Press.

Gillam, T. (2018). *Creativity, wellbeing and mental health practice*. Palgrave Macmillan.

Gipson, L. (2015). Is cultural competence enough? Deepening social justice pedagogy in art therapy. *Art Therapy, 32*(3), 142–145. doi:10.1080/07421656.2015.1060835

Gipson, L. (2019). Envisioning Black women's consciousness in art therapy. In S. K. Talwar (Ed.), *Art therapy for social justice: Radical intersections* (pp. 96–120). Routledge.

Gold, C. (2012). About becoming a music therapist. *Nordic Journal of Music Therapy, 21*(2), 103–105. doi:10.1080/08098131.2012.685271

Gómez Carlier, N., & Salom, A. (2012). When art therapy migrates: The acculturation challenge of sojourner art therapists. *Art Therapy, 29*(1), 4–10. doi:10.1080/0742165 6.2012.648083

Grant, A. M., Berg, J. M., & Cable, D. M. (2014). Job titles as identity badges: How self-reflective titles can reduce emotional exhaustion. *Academy of Management Journal, 57*(4), 1201–1225. doi:10.5465/amj.2012.0338

Guerin, B., & Thain, A. (2018). Attempting to overcome problems shared by both qualitative and quantitative methodologies: Two hybrid procedures to encourage diverse research. *The Australian Community Psychologist, 29*(2), 74–90.

Halstead, R. (2018, January 24). Seniors in San Rafael socialize with new robot. *Marin Independent Journal.* www.marinij.com/general-news/20180124/seniors-in-san-rafael-socialize-with-new-robot

Hargens, L. L. (1990). Variation in journal peer review systems: Possible causes and consequences. *JAMA, 263*(10), 1348–1352. doi:10.1001/jama.1990.03440100052008

Harrington, J. M. (2001). Health effects of shift work and extended hours of work. *Occupational and Environmental Medicine, 58*(1), 68–72. doi:10.1136/oem.58.1.68

Hinz, L. (2009). *Expressive Therapies Continuum: A framework for using art in therapy.* Routledge.

Horn, S. A. (2016). The social and psychological costs of peer review: Stress and coping with manuscript rejection. *Journal of Management Inquiry, 25*(1), 11–26. doi:10.1177/1056492615586597

Howells, V., & Zelnik, T. (2009). Making art: A qualitative study of personal and group transformation in a community arts studio. *Psychiatric Rehabilitation Journal, 32*(3), 215–222. doi:10.2975/32.3.2009.215.222

Huet, V. (2015). Literature review of art therapy-based interventions for work-related stress. *International Journal of Art Therapy: Inscape, 20*(2), 66–76. doi:10.1080/17454832.201 5.1023323

Huet, V. (2017). Case study of an art therapy-based group for work-related stress with hospice staff. *International Journal of Art Therapy: Inscape, 22*(1), 22–34. doi:10.1080 /17454832.2016.1260039

Hyland, K. (2016). Academic publishing and the myth of linguistic injustice. *Journal of Second Language Writing, 31*, 58–69. doi:10.1016/J.JSLW.2016.01.005

Junge, M. B., & Newall, K. (2015). *Becoming an art therapist: Enabling growth, change and action for emerging students in the field.* Charles C. Thomas.

Kaimal, G., Mensinger, J. L., Drass, J. M., & Dieterich-Hartwell, R. M. (2017). Art therapist-facilitated open studio versus coloring: Differences in outcomes of affect, stress, creative agency, and self-efficacy. *Canadian Art Therapy Association Journal, 30*(2), 56–68. doi: 10.1080/08322473.2017.1375827

Kapitan, L. (2015). Social action in practice: Shifting the ethnocentric lens in cross-cultural art therapy encounters. *Art Therapy, 32*(3), 104–111. doi:10.1080/07421656.2015.106 0403

Kleshinski, O., Dunn, T. G., & Kleshinski, J. F. (2010). A preliminary exploration of time management strategies used by physicians in the United States. *International Journal of Medical Education, 1*, 47–54. doi:10.5116/ijme.4c23.117d

Køhlert, F. B. (2019). *Serial selves: Identity and representation in autobiographical comics.* Rutgers University Press.

Kremer, S., Carolan, R., Stafford, K., Partridge, E., & Hill, A. (2016, September). *Getting connected: Research opportunities and exploration for art therapists.* Presentation at Emerging Pathways: New Landscapes in Art Therapy, Berkeley, CA.

Kremer, S., Carolan, R., Stafford, K., Partridge, E., & Hill, A. (2017, November). *Getting connected: Research opportunities and exploration for art therapists*. Panel presentation at Art Therapy: Traversing Landscapes of Heart & Mind, Albuquerque, NM.

Kuther, T. L., & Morgan, R. D. (2020). *Careers in psychology: Opportunities in a changing world* (5th edition). Sage.

Lazar, A., Cornejo, R., Edasis, C., & Piper, A. M. (2016). Designing for the Third Hand: Empowering older adults with cognitive impairment through creating and sharing. *DIS '16: Proceedings of the 2016 ACM Conference on Designing Interactive Systems*, 1047–1058. doi:10.1145/2901790.2901854

LeGette, C. (2017). *Remaking romanticism: The radical politics of the excerpt*. Palgrave Macmillan.

Lightstone, A. J., Bailey, S. K., & Voros, P. (2015). Collaborative music therapy via remote video technology to reduce a veteran's symptoms of severe, chronic PTSD. *Arts and Health, 7*(2), 123–136. doi:10.1080/17533015.2015.1019895

Lindvang, C. (2013). Resonant learning: A qualitative inquiry into music therapy students' self-experiential learning processes. *Qualitative Inquiries in Music Therapy, 8*, 1–30.

Lusebrink, V. B. (2004). Art therapy and the brain: An attempt to understand the underlying processes of art expression in therapy. *Art Therapy, 21*(3), 125–135. doi:10.1080/07421656.2004.10129496

Lusebrink, V. B. (2010). Assessment and therapeutic application of the Expressive Therapies Continuum: Implications for brain structures and functions. *Art Therapy, 27*(4), 168–177. doi:10.1080/07421656.2010.10129380

Mason, J. (2009). Authentic movement: A salve for imposter phenomenon. *Review of Human Factor Studies, 15*(1), 17–32.

McNiff, S. (1992). *Art as medicine: Creating a therapy of the imagination*. Shambhala.

Meier, N., Wegener, C., & Maslo, E. (2018). Editors' introduction: The power of "showing how it happened." In C. Wegener, N. Meier, & E. Maslow (Eds.), *Cultivating creativity in methodology and research: In praise of detours* (pp. 1–7). Palgrave Macmillan.

Merino, C. (2020). Creative pedagogy: Infusing the Ways Paradigm in a foundational course. *Journal of Creativity in Mental Health*. doi:10.1080/15401383.2020.1731397

Miller, G. (2017). *Art therapist's guide to social media: Connection, community, and creativity*. Routledge.

Miserandino, C. (2003). *The Spoon Theory*. Available via https://butyoudontlooksick.com/articles/written-by-christine/the-spoon-theory

Nash, G. (2017). Evaluation and review of art psychotherapy in private practice. *International Journal of Art Therapy, 23*(1), 25–32. doi:10.1080/17454832.2017.1323934

Nolan, E. (2019). Opening art therapy thresholds: Mechanisms that influence change in the community art therapy studio. *Art Therapy, 36*(2), 77–85. doi:10.1080/07421656.2019.1618177

Ostrowski, A., DiPaola, D., Partridge, E., Park, H. W., & Breazeal, C. (2019). Older adults living with social robots: Promoting social connectedness in long-term communities. *IEEE Robotics & Automation Magazine, 26*(2), 59–70. doi:10.1109/MRA.2019.2905234

Owen, J., Thomas, L., & Rodolfa, E. (2013). Stigma for seeking therapy: Self-stigma, social stigma, and therapeutic processes. *The Counseling Psychologist, 41*(6), 857–880. doi:10.1177/0011000012459365

Ozenc, K., & Hagan, M. (2019). *Rituals for work: 50 ways to create engagement, shared purpose, and a culture that can adapt to change*. John Wiley & Sons.

pandaduh (2017, July 22) [Comment on the blog post "Vocational awe"] *WTF Is a Radical Librarian, Anyway?* https://fobaziettarh.wordpress.com/2017/05/30/vocational-awe

Partridge, E. E. (2016a). Access to art and materials: Considerations for art therapists (Accès à l'art et aux matériaux: Facteurs à prendre en compte par les art-thérapeutes). *Canadian Art Therapy Association Journal, 29*(2), 100–104. doi:10.1080/08322473.2016.1252996

Partridge, E. E. (2016b). *Amplified voices: Art-based inquiry into elder communication*. Notre Dame de Namur University.

Partridge, E. E. (2017). *Carving a larger space: Lessons learned from transforming a workplace role*. Presentation at Art Therapy: Traversing Landscapes of Heart & Mind, Albuquerque, NM.

Partridge, E. E. (2019a, February). *Art-based research fieldnotes: Data, biases, bracketing, and inspiration*. Presentation at the 31st Ethnographic & Qualitative Research Conference, Las Vegas, NV.

Partridge, E. E. (2019b, October/November). *Art therapy in the workplace: I'm a therapist but not your therapist*. Presentation at the American Art Therapy Association 50th Annual Conference, Kansas City, MO.

Partridge, E. E. (2019c). *Art therapy with older adults: Connected and empowered*. Jessica Kingsley Publishers.

Partridge, E. E. (2019d, February). *Communicating between media: Back and forth between physical and digital spaces*. Online presentation for the Digital International Creative Arts Therapies Symposium. www.dicats.org

Partridge, E. E. (2019e, July). *Critical conversations: Audience representations in museums*. Presentation at the Social History Curators Group Conference, Edinburgh, Scotland.

Partridge, E. E. (2019f). Dismantling the gender binary in elder care: Creativity instead of craft. In S. Hogan (Ed.), *Gender and difference in the arts therapies: Inscribed on the body* (pp. 196–206). Routledge.

Partridge, E. E. (2019g, November). *Strengthening professional identity and esteem in the creative arts therapies*. Presentation at the Expressive Therapies Summit, New York, NY.

Partridge, E. E., & Jordan, R. (2019, April). *Creative practices in the workplace*. Presentation at the Aging in America Conference, New Orleans, LA.

Pashler, H., McDaniel, M., Rohrer, D., & Bjork, R. (2008). Learning styles: Concepts and evidence. *Psychological Science in the Public Interest, 9*(3), 105–119.

Perry, P. (2010). *Couch fiction: A graphic tale of psychotherapy*. Palgrave Macmillan.

Potash, J. S. (2019). Arts-based research in art therapy. In D. J. Betts & S. P. Deaver (Eds.), *Art therapy research: A practical guide* (pp. 119–146). Routledge.

Reda, M. (2009). *Between speaking and silence: A study of quiet students*. State University of New York Press.

Roca, P. (2016). *Wrinkles*. Fantagraphics Books.

Rolvsjord, R. (2016). Five episodes of clients' contributions to the therapeutic relationship: A qualitative study in adult mental health care. *Nordic Journal of Music Therapy, 25*(2), 159–184. doi:10.1080/08098131.2015.1010562

Sampson, F. (2016). *A speaking likeness: Poetry within health and social care*. Inaugural Wellcome Trust Annual Public Mike White Memorial Lecture.

Saratsi, E., Acot, T., Allinson, E., Edwards, D., Fremantle, C., & Fish, R. (2019). *Valuing arts and arts research*. Valuing Nature Paper 22. Available via https://valuing-nature.net/valuing-arts-and-arts-research

The School of Life, & Microsoft. (n.d.). *Intelligence at work: How successful leaders combine technology with emotional intelligence*. Available via https://resources.office.com/en-landing-WE-M365-CNTNT-FY19-05May-20-Intelligence-at-Work-How-Successful-Leaders-Combine-Technology-with-Emotional-Intelligence-SRGCM1063.html

Skains, R. L. (2018). Creative practice as research: Discourse on methodology. *Journal of Media Practice, 19*(1), 82–98. doi:10.1080/14682753.2017.1362175

Smith, D. (2019). Art therapy draws on place. In R. Hougham, S. Pitruzzella, S. Scoble, & H. Wengrower (Eds.), *Traditions in transition in the arts therapies* (pp. 231–248). University of Plymouth Press.

Sopon, D. (2017). Time management in universities: Best practices and future developments. *Managerial Challenges of the Contemporary Society, 10*(1), 89–94.

Stamm, B. H. (2009). Professional Quality of Life Scale (ProQOL). *I Can, 5*, 1.

Stromstead, T. (2001). Re-inhabiting the female body: Authentic Movement as a gateway to transformation. *The Arts in Psychotherapy, 28*, 39–55.

Talwar, S. K. (2019a). Introduction. In S. K. Talwar (Ed.), *Art therapy for social justice: Radical intersections* (pp. xii–xvi). Routledge.

Talwar, S. K. (2019b). "The sweetness of money": The Creatively Empowered Women (CEW) Design Studio, feminist pedagogy and art therapy. In S. K. Talwar (Ed.), *Art therapy for social justice: Radical intersections* (pp. 178–193). Routledge.

Urwin, J. (2018). Imposter phenomena and experience levels in social work: An initial investigation. *British Journal of Social Work, 48*(5), 1432–1446. doi:10.1093/bjsw/bcx109

Van Lith, T., Fenner, P., & Schofield, M. (2011). The lived experience of art making as a companion to the mental health recovery process. *Disability and Rehabilitation, 33*(8), 652–660. doi:10.3109/09638288.2010.505998

Vogel, D. L., Strass, H. A., Heath, P. J., Al-Darmaki, F. R., Armstrong, P. I., Baptista, M. N., et al. (2017). Stigma of seeking psychological services: Examining college students across ten countries/regions. *Counseling Psychologist, 45*(2), 170–192. doi:10.1177/001100001667141

Waite, M. (2019). Writing medical comics. *Journal of Visual Communication in Medicine, 42*(3), 144–150. doi:10.1080/17453054.2019.1575641

Williams, A., Jones, D., & Robertson, J. (2014). Editorial Introduction. In A. Williams, D. Jones, & J. Robertson (Eds.), *BITE: Recipes for remarkable research* (pp. 2–7). Sense Publishers.

Williams, I. (2015). *The bad doctor: The troubled life and times of Dr Iwan James.* Pennsylvania State University Press.

Williams, I. (2019). Why "Graphic Medicine"? Graphic Medicine. www.graphicmedicine.org/why-graphic-medicine

Wright, S. L., Burt, C. D. B., & Strongman, K. T. (2006). Loneliness in the workplace: Construct definition and scale development. *New Zealand Journal of Psychology, 35*(2), 59–68.

Wrzesniewski, A., Berg, J. M., & Dutton, J. E. (2010, June). Turn the job you have into the job you want. *Harvard Business Review*, 114–117.

Wrzesniewski, A., & Dutton, J. E. (2001). Crafting a job: Revisioning employees as active crafters of their work. *Academy of Management Review, 26*(2), 179–201. doi:10.2307/259118

Index

Rogenski, Kari
advocacy 84, 91
biography of 175–6
collaborations 119, 122–3, 124–5
creative identity 146
deciding on creative arts therapies 13
early career paths 19
early work experiences 49
longevity of creative arts
therapies 155, 169
non-traditional roles 95
non-traditional settings 103
professional identity 113,
114–15, 118, 136
roles in work 72–3
Rohrer, D. 39
roles in work
allies in 77
Andra Duncan 78–9
barriers in 64
building up 65–70
Denise Wolf 71–2
Donna Newman-Bluestein 74, 78
dream work in 74
Erin Partridge 63–70
evolution of 69–70
Fahad al Fahed 75–6
Fatmah Al-Qadfan 77
finances in 63–4
funding applications 75
growth in 71–4
Kari Rogenski 72–3
leadership in 66–7, 77–9
planning for 75–6
privileges in 64
transitions in 67–9
vocational awe 64–5 *see also*
non-traditional roles
Rolvsjord, R. 129

Salom, A. 107
Sampson, F. 60, 110
Saratsi, E. 153
Schofield, M. 130
School of Life 104
self-care 94–5, 143–7
Shimazu, A. 145
Skains, R. L. 152
Smith, D. 109

Sopon, D. 23
Stamm, B. H. 94
stigma 108–9, 160
Sromstead, T. 161
Strongman, K. T. 135–6
supervision 140–1

Talwar, S. K. 40, 100, 129
Thain, A. 153
therapy during training 42–3
Thomas, L. 108
time management 23–4
training programs
academic relationships 43
choosing 33–5
Christine Hirabayashi 38–9
Denise Wolf 45
Donna Newman-Bluestein 38
Fatmah Al-Qadfan 37
Hadas Weissberg 44–5
Jess Minckley 34, 36
Kim Newall 42–3
learning styles 39–41
openness to 37–9
portability of 36
support in 44
therapy during 42–3
transition to work 44–6
work ethic in 41–2
transitions in work roles 67–9

Urwin, J. 115, 116

Van Lith, T. 130
vocational awe 64–5
Vogel, D. L. 108
Voros, P. 127

Waite, M. 56
Weissberg, Hadas
advocacy 90
biography of 176
collaborations 119
creative identity 145, 150
early career paths 17–18
professional identity 116–17,
135, 139, 140–1
transition to work 44–5